CW00818732

Creative Spirits

Creative Spirits

A Toast to Literary Drinkers

John Booth

André Deutsch

First published in 1997 by
André Deutsch
106 Great Russell Street
London WC1B 3LJ

André Deutsch is a subsidiary of VCI plc

This collection copyright © 1997 John Booth

The right of John Booth to be identified
as the author of this work has been asserted
by him in accordance with the Copyright,
Design & Patents Act 1988.

A catalogue record for this title is available
from the British Library

ISBN 0 233 99184 0

Typeset by Derek Doyle & Associates
Mold, Flintshire.
Printed by
St. Edmundsbury Press, Suffolk.

Acknowledgements

The publishers gratefully acknowledge the following for permission to reprint extracts from copyright material.

Kingsley Amis, *Lucky Jim,* by permission of Victor Gollancz; Samuel Beckett, *Murphy*, the Samuel Beckett Estate 1993, published by John Calder Ltd 1963, 1977, Calder Publications 1993, reprinted by permission of the Calder Educational Trust; Hilaire Belloc, *The Path To Rome*, reprinted by permission of the Peters Fraser and Dunlop Group Ltd, on behalf of the Estate of Hilaire Belloc; Anthony Burgess, *The Piano Players*, by permission of Hutchinson Publishers Ltd and the Estate of Anthony Burgess; Colette, *Earthly Paradise*, by permission of Secker & Warburg Publishers; J P Donleavy, *The Ginger Man*, by permission of J P Donleavy; Simone de Beauvoir, *The Prime of Life*, translated by Peter Green (Penguin Books 1965, *La Force de l'Age*, first published in France, 1960) © Librairie Gallimard, 1960, translation © The World Publishing Company; Norman Douglas, *Old Calabria*, by permission of the Society of Authors as the literary representative of the Estate of Norman Douglas; William Faulkner, *Light in August*, by permission of Random House, reproduced by permission of Curtis Brown, London; Scott Fitzgerald, *Tender is the Night*, reprinted by permission of Hardold Ober Associates Inc, © 1933, 1934 by Charles Scribner's Sons, renewed 1961, 1962 by Frances S F Lanahan; Graham Greene, *Brighton Rock*, Heinemann Ltd, by permission of David Higham Associates; Sheila Hodges, *Biography of Lorenzo da Ponte*, by permission of Granada, and imprint of HarperCollins Publishers Ltd; A E Housman, *A Shropshire Lad*, by permission of the Society of Authors; James Joyce, *Ulysses*, by permission of the Estate of James Joyce and Bodley Head; Laurie Lee, *Cider with Rosie*, by permission of Chatto & Windus; Malcolm Lowry, *Under the Volcano*, Jonathan Cape, by permission of the Peters Fraser & Dunlop Group Ltd; Flann O'Brien, *At Swim-Two-Birds*, by permission of HarperCollins Publishers Ltd; Eugene O'Neill, *The Iceman Cometh*, Jonathan Cape, by permission of Random House Ltd; George Orwell, *The Moon Under Water*, © Mark Hamilton as executor of the estate of the late Sonia Brownell Orwell and Martin Secker & Warburg Ltd; J B Priestley, *Outcries and Asides*, William Heinemann Publishers; Jean Rhys, *Tigers Are Better Looking* (Penguin Books, 1972) © Jean Rhys 1962; John Steinbeck, *Cannery Row*, William Heinemann Publishers; Sir John Squire, *Collected Poems*, by permission of Macmillan General Books; Dylan Thomas, *Adventures in the Skin Trade*, J M Dent Publishers, by permission of David Higham Associates; J R R Tolkien, *The Lord of the Rings*, by permission of HarperCollins Publishers Ltd; Evelyn Waugh, *Brideshead Revisited*, reprinted by permission of the Peters Fraser & Dunlop Group.

The publishers apologise for any errors or omissions in this list and would be grateful to be notified of any corrections that should be incorporated into the next edition of this book.

Many people helped in the research for this book, jogged my memory about certain authors, introduced others who were unknown to me. Some were old friends, others strangers, and all were generous in giving their time and help. Among the names I should mention are: David Blount, Jackie Cassell, Scott Goodall, Jay Thompson, Vera Ridley, Roger Bryson, J P Donleavy and the staff of Lewes library.

A complete bibliography of the books I have consulted during the preparation of this book would be impossible because of the space required. I have enjoyed many happy hours of reading, especially a number of fine biographies, and I owe a particular debt of gratitude to the writers of these works.

Contents

Introduction

It is surely unarguable that drink has been as powerful an influence on creative writing as love, philosophy, desire for fame or any other form of inspiration.

The relationship between drink and writing is well established. It is all things to all writers: an encouragement, a support, a solace, a spur, an excuse. For some lucky individuals drink is liberating, galvanizing the imagination to life so the words pour, filling the white emptiness of the page. It can also be effective when coping with that other, more common, part of the writing process: procrastination. This is the time when everything takes precedence over writing: cutting of toenails, filling in fine details on the stubs of chequebooks, attempting to identify a bird perched on a distant tree. The blank page glowers in sullen fashion for days, weeks, even months.The block is rigid, the impasse as solid as a glacier, but it can be broken by the bold writer who escapes to share his frustration – and a glass or three – with other human beings.

It is not at all surprising that the pages of literature are crowded with bibulous characters from Falstaff to Jorrocks because drinking is one of the few principal human activities of which most literary people can claim expert knowledge. Love, passion, carnal knowledge, murder, war, gluttony, jealousy, infidelity, bestiality – some may boast of knowledge of one or other or all of these but it is of drink that most can speak with perfect assurance.

The tradition of literary drinking is long.The Greeks and Romans saw wine as a fruitful influence on poets. For Greek followers of Dionysus, intoxication was a religious experience leading poets to greater understanding of divine mysteries. Roman poets had the same happy idea and any poet worthy of the name was expected to be in his cups most of the time. *In vino veritas* is perhaps the best known of Roman sayings. Plato believed that intoxication revealed the truth of a man's inner self.

A later sage, Doctor Johnson in the eighteenth century made short work of the proposition. Boswell alluded to the maxim, *in vino veritas*, that a man who is well warmed with wine will speak truth. Doctor Johnson, in splendid form, demolished the notion: 'Why, sir, that may be an argument for drinking, if you suppose men in general to be liars. But, sir, I would not keep company with a fellow, who lyes as long as he is sober, and whom you must make drunk before you can get a word of truth out of him.'

Heavy drinking was seen as heroic in the legends of Norse mythology. In Valhalla the dead who had died in battle feasted on an unending supply of strong ale supplied by the goat Heidrun, whose udders never ran dry, and were served by the beautiful Valkyries.

Rabelais, writing in the sixteenth century, looked back to the glorious past: 'Ennius wrote as he drank, drank as he wrote. Aeschylus … used to drink as he composed, to compose as he drank. Homer never wrote on an empty stomach. Cato never wrote except after drinking.' Ronsard echoed the theme: 'As a poet I prefer the good Bacchus to all the other gods.'

It is possible that writers of later centuries were affected, even subconsciously, by these ideas. Until the first half of the twentieth century most educated people were brought up on the classical literature of Greece and Rome and it might be that the seed of the idea linking drinking and creativity was planted in youth.

Simone de Beauvoir claimed that intoxication breaks down the controls and defences that normally protect people against unpalatable truths, forcing them to face reality.

These are issues that are probably best discussed over a few drinks, anyway. What is clear is that drink affects different writers in different ways, just as it does any collection of individuals. There are those whose sole intention is to achieve oblivion; others who loiter over the subtleties of burgundy or claret; some who sample fine whisky or whiskey or take deep and satisfying draughts of amber beer or dark stout.

After spending many months reading and writing about writers and drink, I should be able to show that writers drink more than other people and to explain why they do so. But do writers drink more than butchers, plumbers, schoolmasters, carpenters, and so on? I am not at all sure. What I am sure of is that writers write at length about drinking, as this book amply illustrates.

My purpose in this book is to enjoy the results of the partnership of drink and writers, rather than to establish a link between imbibing and imagination.

There are all manner of writers here: full-blooded, riproaring carousers, wild men of bars and *belles lettres* such as Dylan Thomas and Brendan Behan.Others may be less expected: the aesthete Oscar Wilde who was as handy with a glass as with an epigram, a formidable three-decanter drinker who also had an ungovernable passion for absinthe. James Joyce, who wrote of Guinness with nostalgia in his long exile from Ireland, referring to the 'dull thudding Guinness barrels' being delivered in Dublin. Yet he did not seem unduly worried by his enforced separation from the stout, enjoying fine wines and acquiring a taste for a Swiss white wine which he drank in very large quantities. *Ulysses* is full of references to drinks and pubs, of course, including Bloom's assertion that it would be impossible to cross Dublin on foot without passing the door of a pub. Joyce's compatriot, Flann O'Brien, a notable member of the Dublin drinking scene, expressed in verse the feelings of a typical Dubliner:

When money's tight and hard to get
And your horse has also ran,
When all you have is a heap of debt
A pint of plain is your only man.

Poets loom large in the annals of drinking and have contributed greatly to the literature of drink. Young Keats hymned the 'blushful Hippocrene' and was both enthusiastic and knowledgeable about claret. Alfred Lord Tennyson, that pillar of Victorian rectitude, drank at least a bottle of port at dinner every night, among other things, but was never known to be drunk. Most of the Victorian writers – Thackeray, Trollope, Dickens – drank deeply and celebrated drink in their work.

Modern writers have acquitted themselves well, in reality and fiction. Kingsley Amis was a seasoned, self-confessed toper, holding court at the Garrick after his morning stint at the typewriter. When his first novel, *Lucky Jim*, was read by the publishers, Gollancz, the editor complained that the description of the hero, Jim Dixon, drinking ten or twelve pints in a single session stretched credulity. Amis, with extreme reluctance, reduced the amount to a measly eight pints. His friend of long standing, Philip Larkin, was a prodigious beer drinker in his day and wrote about drink in rather gloomy poetry.

It is impossible to assess the effects of drink on individual writers. Some were highly disciplined, forswearing any drink until the necessary number of words had been produced; others needed a kickstart of alcohol or had to have a bottle handy close to the typewriter.

John Taylor expressed the traditional view in 1637 when he wrote of ale:

> It inspires the poor Poet, who cannot command the price of Canarie or Gascoigne; it mounts the Musician above Eela; it makes the Balladmaker rime beyond Reason; It puts Eloquence into the Oratour; It will make the Philosopher talk profoundly, the Scholler learnedly; and the Lawyer Acute and feelingly.

The Elizabethan Thomas Nashe wrote sharply of the eight kinds of drunkenness, none of them endearing.

> The first is Ape drunke, and he leapes, and sings, and hollowes, and daunceth for the heauens: the second is Lion drunke, and he flings the pots about the house, calls his hostess whore, breaks the glass windowes with his dagger, and is apt to quarrell with any man that speaks to him: the third is Swine drunke, heavy, lumpish and sleepie, and cries for a little more drinke, and a few more cloathes; the fourth is Sheep drunke, wise in his own concept, when he cannot bring foorth a right word; the fifth is Mawdlen drunke, when a fellow will weepe for kindness in the midst of his Ale and kiss you, saying; By God Captaine I loue thee, goe thy waies thou dost not thinke so often of me as I do of thee, I would (if it pleased God) could I not loue thee so well as I doo, and then he puts his finger in his eie, and cries; the sixth is Martin drunke when a man is drunke and drinker himselfe sober ere he stirre: the seuenth is Goate drunke, when in his drunkennese he hath no mind but upon Lechery: the eighth is Foxe drunke, when he craftie drunke, as many of the Dutch men bee, will neuer bargaine but when they are drunke.

Nashe was a pretty shrewd observer and it is clear that times have not changed greatly since the same characters are recognizable to anybody familiar with drinkers. Despite his view of drinkers in general, however, Nashe seemed to view scholars as being in a different category altogether.

> Give a Scholler wine, going to his Booke, or being about to invent, it sets a new Poynt on his wit, it glazeth it, it Scowres it, it gives him Acumen.

Readers may judge for themselves how our selection of writers performed with glass and pen through the centuries and may agree with that apostle of sound common sense, J B Priestley, when he wrote:

> Drunkenness in good literature is not like drunkenness in real life; it is subtly spiritualised; the sparkle, bloom, and fragrance of wine, the jolly comradeship of the bottle, the Bacchic ardours and ecstasies, are all there, without the hiccoughs and the carbuncles, the sagging mouth and the shaking hands.

Inflamed By Drink

Goate drunke, when in his drunkennese he hath no mind but upon Lechery.

Thomas Nashe

Sir George Etherege

Among his many claims to fame as playwright, poet and man of fashion, Sir George Etherege has the added distinction of being included in a group which, according to Bishop Wilberforce, 'still maintain a bad pre-eminence in the annals of English vice'.

It was no mean achievement on the part of Etherege to achieve such eminence in the Restoration, when the King himself set a challenging standard in licentious behaviour for his court to follow. The group with which Etherege was associated included some of the most gifted, as well as the most scandalous, names of the period – Rochester and Buckingham, Sedley and Killigrew. Rakes, every one of them, but men who were as graceful in pursing a fashionable, preferably virtuously married beauty, as penning a poem or delivering an epigram.

Etherege's love of drink was probably not as powerful as his love of women, though both were considerable. He knew the value of drink, quoting a proverb current at the time: 'Truth is in ale as in history.'

It is appropriate that champagne was the popular drink of the gallants during most of his lifetime. Sparkling champagne was a new drink then, an invention credited, not entirely credibly, to Dom Perignon, cellarer at the abbey of Hautvilliers. The court loved it and it seemed to epitomize the life of that gaudy, bawdy period. In *She Would if She Could*, the playwright Etherege refers to it:

> Drink thy flask of Champaign,
> 'Twill serve you for paint and love potion.

His plays deal in a witty, good-natured fashion with seduction, cuckolding and drinking. But, though lighthearted, there is a deal of wisdom in his observations, as on drink in a letter to his old friend and fellow libertine, the Duke of Buckingham, dated 12 November 1688.

> To unbosom myself frankly and freely to your Grace, I always looked upon Drunkenness to be an unpardonable crime in a young Fellow, who, without any of the foreign Helps, has Fire

> enough in his veins to do Justice to Coelia whenever she demands a Tribute from him. In a middle-aged Man, I consider the Bottle as only subservient to the Nobler Pleasure of Love; and he that would suffer himself to be so far infatuated by it, as to neglect the Pursuit of a more agreeable Game, I think deserves no Quarter from the ladies. In old Age, indeed, when it is convenient to forget and steal from ourselves, I am of opinion that a little Drunkenness, discreetly used, may as well contribute to our Health of Body as Tranquillity of Soul.

If Rochester takes the palm for excessive drinking (his claim never to have been sober for five years was never challenged), Etherege is probably the leader of the group in matters of style. He said, 'I am a fop in my heart. I have been so used to affection, that without the help of the court, what is natural cannot touch me.' To him, the cut of a coat or the set of a periwig was as important as a poem. His writings aimed only to entertain, to give pleasure. Plays such as *She Would if She Could* and *The Man of Mode* did just that.

He is as one with his characters – indeed, he was probably drawing on himself when creating Dorimant in *The Man of Mode*. Etherege was an assiduous and successful womanizer, a collector of beauties from the stage and court. It was said he married to obtain a knighthood or obtained a knighthood to marry into money. Certainly, his marriage does not appear to have been one made in heaven and had a positively brittle tone. His letters to his wife are brisk, businesslike and generally concerned with money. They are icily polite, as in his signing off in one letter with:

> I will no more subscribe myself your loving since you take it ill, but
> Madame,
>
> Your most most dutiful husband. G E

The Man of Mode

OLD BELLAIR The women are all gone to bed, – Fill, boy! – Mr Medley, begin a health.
MEDLEY (*whispers*) To Emilia.
OLD BELLAIR Out a prize! She's a rogue, and I'll not pledge you.

MEDLEY I know you will.
OLD BELLAIR Adod, drink it then!
SIR FOPLING Let us have the new bachique.
OLD BELLAIR Adod, that is a hard word! What does it mean, sir?
MEDLEY A catch or drinking song.
OLD BELLAIR Let us have it, then.
SIR FOPLING Fill the glasses round, and draw up in a body – Hey, music!
They sing

The pleasures of love and the joys of good wine,
To perfect our happiness wisely we join.
We to beauty all day
Give the sovereign sway
And her favourite nymphs devoutly obey.
At the plays we are constantly making our court,
And when they are ended, we follow the sport
To The Mall and the Park,
Where we love till 'tis dark,
Then sparkling Champaign
Puts an end to their reign;
It quickly recovers
Poor languishing lovers,
Makes us frolic and gay, and drowns all sorrow;
But alas, we relapse again on the morrow.
Let every man stand
With his glass in his hand,
And briskly discharge at the word of command.
Here's a health to all those
Whom we tonight depose.
Wine and beauty by turns great souls should inspire;
Present all together – and now, boys, give fire!

Henry Fielding

The enthusiastic debauchery of Henry Fielding's most famous character, Tom Jones, was shared and even surpassed by his creator.

Fielding was, by general agreement, a spendthrift, a drunkard and a lecher. A strapping fellow of a lively disposition and blessed with a fortunately robust constitution, he was not, however, a particularly attractive individual because of his devotion to drink. He could almost always be seen carrying a glass while dribbles of tobacco juice – tobacco chewing was yet another of his questionable habits – ran from the corners of his mouth.

But he was brilliant. When still in his twenties, his comedies won him fame and fortune. Dean Swift, who claimed he had laughed but twice in his life, stated that one of those occasions was during a play by Fielding.

He wrote from life, as a friend remarked: 'Had his life been less regular (for irregular it was, and spent in promiscuous intercourse with persons of all ranks) his pictures of humankind had been neither as various nor so natural.' For Fielding, his plays were merely a means of obtaining money to satisfy his many pleasures. It was said of him that 'whatever he desired, he desired ardently' and it was his character to 'catch at every hook pleasure baited'.

Fielding had another life far from the stewpots of London; that of a country gentleman in rural Dorset where he mixed with local society, rode to hounds and drank mightily. It was from these times that many of the characters who appeared in *Tom Jones* and *Joseph Andrews* sprang.

His indulgent habits remained throughout his life, certainly as far as drink was concerned (it is possible that age affected his womanizing but there is insufficient evidence on this score), continuing throughout his years as a famous author and his later work as a lawyer and magistrate.

It is not altogether surprising that even his constitution failed in time. He became a martyr to gout and other ailments. Yet, even towards the end of his life, he remained convivial describing what he required in a companion 'with as much of the Qualifications of Learning, Sense, and Good Humour as you can find, who will drink a moderate Glass in an Evening or will at least sit with me 'till one when I do.'

His finest epitaph came from his kinswoman, Lady Mary Wortley Montagu, who said 'no man enjoyed life more than he did'. She went on, speaking with the authority of familiarity: 'His happy constitution (even when he had, with great pains, half demolished it) made him forget everything when he was before a venison pasty or over a glass of Champaign; and I am persuaded he has known more happy moments than any prince upon earth.'

The History of Tom Jones

It was now a pleasant evening in the latter end of June, when our hero was walking in a most delicious grove, where the gentle breezes fanning the leaves, together with the sweet trilling of a murmuring stream, and the melodious notes of nightingales, formed altogether the most enchanting harmony. In this scene, so sweetly accommodated to love, he meditated on his dear Sophia. While his wanton fancy roamed unbounded over all her beauties, and his lively imagination painted the charming maid in various ravishing forms, his warm heart melted with tenderness; and at length, throwing himself on the ground, by the side of a gently murmuring brook, he broke forth into the following ejaculation:

'O Sophia, would Heaven give thee to my arms, how blest would be my condition! Curst be that fortune which sets a distance between us. Was I but possessed of thee, one only suit of rags thy whole estate, is there a man on earth whom I could envy! How contemptible would the brightest Circassian beauty, drest in all the jewels of the Indies, appear to my eyes! But why do I mention another woman? Could I think my eyes capable of looking at any other with tenderness, these hands should tear them from my head. No, my Sophia, if cruel fortune separates us for ever, my soul shall doat on thee alone. The chastest constancy will I ever preserve to thy image. Though I should never have possession of thy charming person, still shalt thou alone have possession of my thoughts, my love, my soul. Oh! my fond heart is so wrapt in that tender bosom, that the brightest beauties would for me have no charms, nor would a hermit be colder in their embraces. Sophia, Sophia alone shall be mine. What raptures are in that name! I will engrave it on every tree.'

At these words he started up, and beheld – not his Sophia – no, nor a Circassian maid richly and elegantly attired for the grand Signior's seraglio. No; without a gown, in a shift that was somewhat of the coarsest, and none of the cleanest, bedewed likewise with some odoriferous effluvia, the produce of the day's labour, with a pitchfork in her hand, Molly Seagrim approached. Our hero had his penknife in his hand, which he had drawn for the before-mentioned purpose of carving on the bark; when the girl coming near him, cryed out with a smile, 'You don't intend to kill me, squire, I hope!' – 'Why should you think I would kill you?' answered Jones. 'Nay', replied she 'after your cruel usage of me when I saw you last, killing me would, perhaps, be too great kindness for me to expect.'

Here ensued a parley, which, as I do not think myself obliged to relate it, I shall omit. It is sufficient that it lasted a full quarter of an hour, at the conclusion of which they retired into the thickest part of the grove.

Some of my readers may be inclined to think this event unnatural. However, the fact is true; and perhaps may be sufficiently accounted for by suggesting, that Jones probably thought one woman better than none, and Molly as probably imagined two men to be better than one. Besides the before-mentioned motive assigned to the present behaviour of Jones, the reader will be likewise pleased to recollect in his favour that he was not at this time perfect master of that wonderful power of reason, which so well enables grave and wise men to subdue their unruly passions, and to decline any of these prohibited amusements. Wine now had totally subdued this power in Jones. He was, indeed, in a condition, in which, if reason had interposed, though only to advise, she might have received the answer which one Cleostratus gave many years ago to a silly fellow, who asked him, if he was not ashamed to be drunk? 'Are not you,' said Cleostratus, 'ashamed to admonish a drunken-man?' To say the truth, in a court of justice drunken-ness must not be an excuse, yet in a court of conscience it is greatly so; and therefore Aristotle, who commends the laws of Pittacus, by which drunken men received double punishment for their crimes, allows there is more of policy than justice in that law. Now, if there are any transgressions pardonable from drunkenness, they are certainly such as Mr Jones was a present guilty of; on which head I could pour forth a vast profusion of learning, if I imagined it would either entertain my reader, or teach him anything more than he knows already. For his sake therefore I shall keep my learning to myself.

Graham Greene

Graham Greene

Graham Greene was a man who plunged rather than fell into temptation, whether it was drinking, drugs or sex. Drink was not, however, as powerful a preoccupation as sex, not quite.

Drinking, heavy drinking, was a part of his life. At Oxford he excelled in the traditional undergraduate pursuits of drinking and idling. He even made an attempt to emulate his hero, Lord Rochester – who boasted of never being sober for five years – and claimed at least a measure of success by being drunk for a term. His cronies, the gilded, glittering bright young things who were to become the literary establishment of the future, delighted in heavy drinking and elaborate jokes. Typical japes included dressing up as Arabs and walking around the countryside in rags pushing a barrel organ.

Drinking, like drugs and probably sex, was an escape from his greatest enemy, boredom. There was plenty of boredom and plenty of drinking during his war years as an espionage agent in Africa.

Most of Greene's reminiscences refer at some point to his excessive drinking but, of course, such drinking was common in the circles in which he moved: especially among publishers and journalists. All agree he had a strong head, as he said himself.

His taste in drink was happily catholic. He liked pubs and most types of drink. One of his many lovers, Jocelyn Rickards, is quoted by Michael Shelden in his less than reverential biography of Greene:

> I consumed in our time more oysters and smoked salmon, champagne, Black Velvet or Pouilly Fumee than I have swallowed in the rest of my life.

He seems to have enjoyed unusual drinks, especially when they were highly alcoholic. A gift of 94 per cent gin was appreciated, with a request for more. In China he discovered a liking for Mou-Tai, a wine (described as tasting like a mixture of petrol and vodka) with an alcoholic content of 50 per cent.

Neither his lifelong taste for alcohol nor any of his other excesses appears to have affected the quality or the quantity of his work. He died, still drinking and working, at the age of 87.

Brighton Rock

He watched her with scared lust. She had belonged to Spicer: her voice had wailed up the telephone wires making assignations: he had received letters in mauve envelopes, addressed to him: even Spicer had had something to be proud of, to show to friends – 'my girl'. He remembered some flowers which had come to Frank's labelled 'Broken-hearted'. He was fascinated by her infidelity. She belonged to nobody – unlike a table or a chair. He said slowly, putting his arm round her to take her glass and pressing her breast clumsily, 'I'm going to be married in a day or two.' It was as if he were staking a claim to his share of infidelity: he wasn't to be beaten by experience. He lifted her glass and drank it. The sweetness dripped down his throat, his first alcohol touched the palate like a bad smell: this was what people called pleasure – this and the game. He put his hand on her thigh with a kind of horror: Rose and he: forty-eight hours after Prewitt had arranged things: alone in God knows what apartment – what then, what then? He knew the traditional actions as a man may know the principles of gunnery in chalk on a blackboard, but to translate the knowledge to action, to the smashed village and the ravaged woman, one needed help from the nerves. His own were frozen with repulsion: to be touched, to give oneself away, to lay oneself open – he had held intimacy back as long as he could at the end of a razor blade.

He said, 'Come on. Let's dance.'

They circulated slowly in the dance hall. To be beaten by experience was bad enough, but to be beaten by greenness and innocence, by a girl who carried plates at Snow's, by a little bitch of sixteen years ...

'Spicie thought a lot of you,' Sylvie said.

'Come out to the cars,' the Boy said.

'I couldn't, not with Spicie dead only yesterday.'

They stood and clapped and then the dance began again. The shaker clacked in the bar, and the leaves of one small tree were pressed against the window beyond the big drum and the saxophone ...

... 'Come to the cars.'

'Poor Spicie,' but she led the way, and he noticed with uneasiness how she ran – literally ran – across the lit corner of what had once been a farmyard towards the dark car-park and the game. He thought with sickness, 'In three minutes I shall know.'

'Which is your car?'

'That Morris.'

'No good to us,' Sylvie said. She darted down the line of cars. 'This Ford.' She pulled the door open, said, 'Oh pardon me,' and shut it, scrambled into the back of the next car in the line and waited for him. 'Oh', her voice softly and passionately pronounced from the dim interior, 'I love a Lancia.' He stood in the doorway and the darkness peeled away between him and the fair and vacuous face. Her skirt drawn up above her knees she waited for him with luxurious docility.

Guy de Maupassant

Guy de Maupassant is more famous for his exploits with whores – exploits mirrored in such tales as 'Boule de Suif' and 'Le Maison Tellier' – than his exploits with wine, but he was a drinker of note.

Maupassant had a prodigious appetite for all experiences that normally engage the interests of vigorous, hot-blooded men. In his youth he was an outstanding oarsman, capable of rowing 50 miles a day along the Seine. According to a friend, his blood 'boiled in his veins like sap'. There were plenty of opportunities for releasing his fiery energy, particularly at La Grenouillère, the floating cabaret made famous in the paintings of Renoir and Monet. Maupassant painted the scene as vividly in words in his short story, 'Yvette':

> An immense roofed barge, moored to the bank, was laden with a mass of men and women eating and drinking at tables, or standing about shouting, singing, dancing, capering to the sound of a throbbing, tinny old piano.
>
> A number of large, red-lipped, red-headed foul-mouthed girls were walking undulating their bustles and their buttocks and eyeing everyone in invitation. Others were dancing madly with half-naked young men in rowing clothes and jockey caps. The whole place smelled of sweat and face powder, of perfume and armpits. The drinkers at the tables were downing liquors of all colours – white, red, yellow and green; and there were shouting

and yelling for no reason except a violent need to make a noise, a purely animal necessity.

Later, when writing for the fashionable and irreverent journal *Gil-Blas*, Maupassant and his friends floated in a sea of champagne and debauchery. A prominent member of the staff was a baron who devoted himself to organizing champagne parties and fencing exhibitions with the assistance of a young man known as 'The Intrepid Bottle-opener' who was the paper's gossip editor and had the useful second string of being a champagne salesman.

As is well known, Maupassant suffered from his enthusiasm for women, for what his mentor Flaubert described as 'too many whores'. It might have been better for him if he had been more single-minded in pursuit of drink, although there is nothing halfhearted in his jocular, Rabelaisian letter to a friend about drinking and other pursuits at La Grenouillère.

Letter

After a goodly number of aperitifs, we began our feast by consuming 2,591 bottles of wine of Argenteuil, 678 bottles of good wine of Bordeaux, 746 bottles of Pommard, and 27,941 hogsheads of Ay. Thereupon we commenced to feel of good cheer. But ill accustomed to our Pantagruelian repasts, that old f— La Toque commenced to roll his eyes in such an odd and grievous manner, followed by his belly rolling even more grievously, that he at last fell to the floor and henceforth stirred no more.

At this we mopped him and washed him and rubbed him, hoisted him and carried him and undressed him and laid him out, completely besoused; thereupon we recited at his bedside the prayers and orisons of loafers, tipplers, wine-bibbers and the like with the effect that he slept, snored, made exceeding wind all night long and awakened stiff and aching and cold: head, neck, back, chest, arms and everything.

And the morror we did begin again. Now the day whereon God the Father rested after creating both heaven and earth, we arrived at Bezons. And that day Prunier did many things, feats of navigation most astonishing, marvellous and superlative, such as to row from Bezons as far as Argenteuil a sailing ship so frightfully large that he thought he had left the skin of his hands upon the oars (two beautiful whores were in said sailing ship).

Ovid

A reading of Ovid's *Ars Amatoria* (*The Art of Love*) explains why so many people remain devoted to him; the work is sensual, realistic and elegantly rude.

Ovid was born in a small town 90 miles from Rome in the time of Augustus. He came from a well-born family and enjoyed a wide education which included a visit to Athens. He appears to have had no need to pursue a career and spent his time in writing witty, mildly erotic poetry, of which *Ars Amatoria* is a fine example.

His tone is worldly rather than cynical and his advice, even to twentieth-century ears, seems eminently sensible. In the first book of *Ars Amatoria* he is counselling men on winning their lady-loves. There are, he says, opportunities at banquets where wine will be present for it 'makes men apt for passion'.

In the third book Ovid addresses women on matters of love in a long and surprisingly detailed account of how women can make themselves more successful in winning lovers, including make-up and the best positions to adopt for sexual intercourse.

On avoiding the temptations of love brought about by drink, Ovid is brisk: abstinence or excess:

> Wine prepares the heart for love, unless you take o'ermuch and your spirits are dulled and drowned by too much liquor. By wind is a fire fostered, and by wind extinguished; a gentle breeze fans the flame, a strong breeze kills it. Either no drunkenness, or so much as to banish care: aught between these two is harmful.

> Often has bright-hued Love with soft arms drawn to him and embraced the horns of Bacchus as he there reclined: and when wine has sprinkled Cupid's thirsty wings, he abides and stands o'erburdened, where he has taken his place ... Wine gives courage and makes men apt for passion; care flees and is drowned in much wine. Then laughter comes, then even the poor find

plenty, then sorrow and care and the wrinkles of the brow depart ... At such time often have women bewitched the minds of men, and Venus in the wine has been fire in fire. Trust not at such a time o'ermuch to the treacherous lamp; darkness and drink impair your judgement of beauty.

He has wise words on drinking:

Better suited is drinking, and were more becoming in a woman: not badly goest thou, Bacchus, with Venus' son. This too note, when the head endures, the mind and feet are also firm; do not see double where there is but one. A woman lying steeped in wine is an ugly sight; she deserves to endure any union whatever. Nor is it safe when the table is cleared to fall asleep; in sleep much happens that is shameful.

Ars Amatoria

Therefore when the bounty of Bacchus set before you falls to your lot, and a woman shares your convivial couch, beseech the Nictelian sire and the spirits of the night that they bid not the wines to hurt your head. Here may you say many things lurking in covered speech, so that she may feel they are said to her, and you may trace light flatteries in thin characters of wine, that on the table she may read herself your mistress; you may gaze at her eyes with eyes that confess their flame: there are often voice and words in a silent look. See that you are the first to seize the cup her lips have touched, and drink at that part where she has drunk; and whatever food she has touched with her fingers see that you ask for, and while you ask contrive to touch her hand. Let it also be your aim to please your lady's husband; he is often more useful to you, if made a friend. To him, if you drink by lot, concede the first turn; give him the garland tossed from your own head. Whether he be below you or hold an equal place, let him take of all before you; nor hesitate to yield him place in talk. 'Tis a safe and oft-trodden path, to deceive under the name of friend; safe and oft-trodden though it be, 'tis the path of guilt. Thus too an agent pursues his agency too far and looks after more than was committed to his charge ...

Alexander Pope

Pope suffered greatly from the inevitable excesses of life as a gentleman of fashion. He was physically ill-equipped for drinking and debauchery, being only 4½ feet tall and sickly, but he had considerable determination. At one time he regularly stayed up until the small hours over burgundy and champagne and regretted being, 'So much a modern rake that I shall be ashamed … to be thought to do any business.'

In December 1713 he complained of being 'in great disorder with sickness at my head and stomach', after drinking with other wits and men of fashion. His old friend Sir George Turnbull warned him about his habits: 'to get out of all tavern-company. What a misery it is for you to be destroyed by the foolish kindness … of those who are able to bear the poison of bad wine, and to engage you in so unequal a contest.'

Certainly, the contest was unequal when he drank with Addison at the Lion Hotel at Hampton. It is said poor Pope was left in such disorder that he denounced Addison for months afterwards as a terrible drunkard, which was not entirely untrue. Of course, it can be said there was no better man than Pope at bearing a grudge, as can be seen from the *Dunciad*, in which some 100 friends and foes are pilloried.

It would have been difficult, in any case, to refuse invitation as charming and persuasive as that from Lord Lansdowne, who promised, 'I can give you no Falernum that has outlived twenty consulships, but I can promise you a bottle of good old claret that has seen two reigns.'

Pope delighted in the society of such people. One of them, Viscount Bolingbroke – politician, courtier, lecher – recorded a day of huge fulfilment: 'as the happiest man alive, got drunk, harangued the Queen, and at night was put to bed to a beautiful young lady, and was tucked up by two of the prettiest young peers in England.'

Another of Pope's weaknesses in the matter of drink was his dangerous habit of writing unseemly letters when he was a little tipsy, which was often. In November 1714 he was clearly inflamed with passion and alcohol when he wrote to a lady, ''Tis some proof of my sincerity towards you that I write when I am prepared by drinking to speak truth … Wine awakens and refreshes the lurking passions of the mind, as varnish does the colours that are sunk in a picture, and brings them all out in their natural glowings.'

According to Dr Johnson, in insufferably pompous vein when considering his own habits, Pope was 'one of those who, suffering much pain, think themselves entitled to whatever pleasure they can snatch. He was too indulgent to his appetite.'

The Wife of Bath's Prologue from The Canterbury Tales

Thus with my first three Lords I past my Life;
A very Woman, and a very Wife!
What Sums from these old Spouses I cou'd raise,
Procur'd young Husbands in my riper Days.
Tho' past my Bloom, not yet decay'd was I,
Wanton and wild, and chatter'd like a Pye.
In Country Dances still I bore the Bell,
And sung as sweet as Evening *Philomel*,
To clear my Quail-pipe, and refresh my Soul,
Full oft I drain'd the Spicy Nut-brown Bowl;
Rich luscious Wines, that youthful Blood improve,
And warm the swelling Veins to Feats of Love;
For 'tis as sure as Cold ingenders Hail,
A Liqu'rish Mouth must have a Lech'rous Tail;
Wine lets no Lover unrewarded go,
As all true Gamesters by Experience know.
But oh good Gods! when'er a Thought I cast
On all the Joys of Youth and Beauty past,
To find in Pleasure I have had my Part.

Lord Rochester

John Wilmot, Earl of Rochester, is remembered today for his confession towards the end of his life that he had not been sober for the past five years. From all the evidence, it seems clear he was guilty of a gross understatement.

Lord Rochester was a notorious libertine in an age noted for its excesses. A favourite of King Charles II, he was given the appropriate office of Gentleman of the King's Bedchamber and shared the favours of a number of the King's mistresses, although his catholic sexual tastes ranged from ladies of fashion to street-corner whores. His amorous and obscene verses were widely admired, although some incurred royal disapproval and banishment from the court, such as:

> Restless he rolls about from whore to whore,
> A merry monarch, scandalous and poor.
> Nor are his high desires above his strength;
> His sceptre and his Prick are of a length.

Rochester's charm and wit ensured his absence was brief. He was at his best in his cups, as the historian Gilbert Burnet noted: 'The natural heat of his fancy being inflamed by wine, made him so extravagantly pleasant, that many, to be more diverted by that humour, studied to engage him deeper and deeper in intemperance.'

There was a savage side to his humour, as in the lampoon on one of the King's mistresses, Barbara Villiers, Duchess of Cleveland and Countess of Castlemaine who, the poet wrote:

> I say is much to be admired,
> Although she ne'er was satisfied or tired.
> Full forty men a day
> Provided for this whore,
> Yet like a bitch she wags her tail for more.

The spirited and salacious correspondence with his friend, Henry Savile, provides much information about Rochester's approach to life. It was to Savile that he wrote, 'I have seriously consider'd one thing, that the three businesses of this age, women, politics, and drinking, the last is the only exercise at which you and I have not prov'd ourselves arrant fumblers.'

And Savile was the target of this extravagant appeal:

> Do a charity becoming one of your pious principles, in preserving your humble servant Rochester from the imminent peril of sobriety; which, for want of good wine more than company (for I can drink like a hermit betwixt God and my own conscience) is very

like to befall me. Remember what pains I have formerly taken to wean you from your pernicious resolutions of discretion and wisdom! And, if you have a grateful heart (which is a miracle amongst you statesmen), show it, by directing the bearer to the best wine in town; and pray let not this highest point of sacred friendship be perform'd lightly, but go about it with all due deliberation and care, as holy priests to sacrifice, or as discreet thieves to the wary performance of burglary and shop-lifting. Let your well-discerning palate (the best judge about you) travel from cellar to cellar, and then from piece to piece, till it has lighted on wine fit for its noble choice and my approbation.

It is no great surprise that Rochester's life was short. He died, as Graham Greene observed, at 33, of old age.

The Debauchee

I rise at eleven, dine about two,
I get drunk before seven, and the next thing I do,
I send for my whore, when for fear of the clap,
I dally about her and spew in her lap;
There we quarrel and scold till I fall asleep,
When the jilt growing bold, to my pocket does creep;
Then slyly she leaves me, and to revenge the affront,
At once both my lass and my money I want.
If by chance then I awake, hot-heated and drunk,
What a coy do I make for the loss of my punk?
I storm, and I roar, and I fall in a rage,
And missing my lass, I fall on my page:
Then crop-sick, all morning I rail at my men,
And in bed I lie yawning till eleven again.

Upon His Drinking Bowl

Vulcan contrive me such a Cup
As Nestor used of old;
Shew all the skill to trim it up,
Damask it round with Gold.

But carve thereon a spreading Vine,
Then add Two Lovely Boys,
Their Limbs in Amorous fold intwine
The Type of future Joys.

Cupid, and Bacchus, my Saints are,
May drink, and Love, still reign,
With Wine, I wash away my cares,
And then to Cunt again.

Anthony Burgess

Anthony Burgess, as he would have been the first to admit, knew everything. With the possible exception of George Steiner, an exception with which Burgess would not have agreed, he seemed to know more than anyone in the world.

Many people were put off by his booming self-confidence, by what some saw as his over-weening self-regard, but Burgess had the infuriating gall to be right. He knew everything that was worth knowing, in a number of fields at least. Novelist, poet, commentator, philologist, composer; the list of his accomplishments is long and impressive. He was also a lifelong and enthusiastic drinker.

He came from a hard school of Northern drinkers and was inordinately proud of his provincial roots (though like many proud provincials, he was careful to spend most of his life far from his native heath, in his case the city of Manchester, while declaring the utmost affection for the place.)

At a late age he remembered the days of his youth and getting drunk on five pints of strong bitter beer at sixpence a pint. During the war he became acquainted with the drunken literati of Fitzrovia: Dylan Thomas, George Orwell and countless others. Pubs such as The Wheatsheaf, The Black Horse and The Duke of York were milestones on long drunken evenings.

His autobiography (only two volumes, surprisingly) is littered with accounts of drinking by himself and with his first wife, in Britain and abroad, on land and at sea. Teaching in Malaya led to a transfer from the beer and cider of Britain to a diet of gin and local brews such as 'todi' which 'stank of vegetable decay ... you had to plug your nose while you drank it.'

Burgess clearly had a strong head or sound liver, his wife did not and suffered in consequence. Physically tough, he was also industrious and prolific, producing book after book and gaining literary eminence.

Back in England, they lived for many years in the rather drab Sussex village of Etchingham, where Burgess felt his reputation as a writer was unappreciated by the locals, although there was a literary clan, presumably known to him, in nearby Longford. A local remembers him at this period in the village pub – always in the saloon, never the public bar – announcing in a ringing voice to an admiring circle: 'I write a thousand words a day. A thousand polished words.'

He is also recalled playing the piano for a TV film crew at his home, large gin on top of the piano. Every now and then Burgess would stop playing, drain the glass with a single gulp and continue playing.

He became a public figure, a celebrity, welcomed on television chat shows, a prolific reviewer in the serious press, even managing to give a favourable review to one of his own books on one occasion. There were trips to America, to Russia, still more drink and still more work. He was still working when he died, and drinking, but still superbly comfortable in the role of polymath.

The Piano Player

But the draught Bass and whisky in my dad was having a new effect now, and he began to doze off with his fingers just trailing along the keys.

'Dad, dad, wake up. Come on, let me get you home.' Oh God, it was a proper bloody mess. I couldn't help looking to see how much of this the audience was taking in, and what I saw was the manager Hawkes coming down the aisle very heavy footed. 'Dad, dad, for God's sake,' He came to then, smacking his lips, which must have been very dry, squinted up at the screen and said:

'Who's that bugger there then?'

I squinted up too and could make out this bearded man leering and counting money he was pouring from a bag into his hand.

'Judas, dad.'

'Judas, right.' And he began to play very severe solemn chords, and I thought thank God and went to sit down again. Hawkes was there now, leaning over me and his breath very sour with beer and saying:

'What's going on here? What the hell's bloody well up?'

'Don't you use words like that to me,' I said. 'Especially with this film on about Our Lord,' I said then. Then my father began to sing a new waltz song he was making up as he went along, doing big runs up and down the keyboard:

Thiiiiiiirty pieces of silver,
That's what I sold him for.
Thiiiiiiirty pieces of silver,
I am the son of a whore.

Ernest Hemingway

Perhaps Hemingway's greatest problem was that he was the hero of his own life. He could not imagine, or invent, a finer, bigger, more capable man – one who could outfight, outfuck and outdrink any man, alive or dead.

He clearly regarded drinking as a skill, like being good with a gun or pen. It was and remained one of the great pleasures of his life. 'I like to see every man drunk. A man does not exist until he is drunk … I love getting drunk. Right from the start it is the best feeling.'

Hemingway believed his vigorous sporting lifestyle, of boxing, tennis, game fishing and hunting, burned off the effects of the alcohol. Perhaps they did, because for a long time he suffered few adverse effects from the prodigious amounts of alcohol he consumed. As he said: 'Those famous three or four bottle men were living all the time in the open air – hunting, shooting, always on a horse. In that life as in skiing or fishing you can drink any amount'.

He was unashamed in his pleasure in drink: 'I have drunk since I was fifteen and few things have given me more pleasure. When you work hard all day with your head and know you must work again the next day what else can change your ideas and make them run on a different plane like whisky? When you're cold and wet what else can warm you? Before an attack who can say anything that gives you the momentary well being that rum does? I would as soon not eat at night as not to have red wine and water.'

Jordan in *For Whom The Bell Tolls* is surely the author when he speaks poetically of absinthe:

> One cup of it took the place of the evening papers, all of the old evenings in cafes, of all chestnut trees that would be in bloom now in this month, of the great slow horses of the puter boulevards, of bookshops, of kiosks, and of galleries, of the Parc Mountsouris, of the Stade Buffalo, and of the Butte Chaumont ... and of being able to read and relax in the evening; of all the things he had enjoyed and forgotten and that came back to him when he tasted that opaque, bitter, tongue-numbing, brain-warming, stomach-warming, idea-changing liquid alchemy

Papa Hemingway, as he became known, set the house record for the number of double daiquiris drunk in a single session at the Hotel Floridita, in Havana. The hero of *Islands in the Stream*, is another case of Hemingway thinly disguised:

> He had drunk double frozen daiquiris, the great ones that Constante made, that had no taste of alcohol and felt, as you drank them, the way downhill skiing feels running through powder snow and, after the sixth and eighth, felt like downhill glacier skiing feels when you are running unroped.

Hemingway always claimed he was not what he described as 'a rummy', insisting that he controlled his drinking. He usually said he remained sober while drinking, but his lifestyle puts a questions mark over that statement.

In an interview with the *Paris Review* in 1954 he recalled that he wrote six stories in one day in Madrid, with the help of a great deal of booze.

> First I wrote *The Killers*, which I'd tried to write before and failed. Then after lunch I got in bed to keep warm and wrote Today is Friday. I had so much juice I thought maybe I was going crazy and I had about six other stories to write. So I got dressed and walked to Fornos, the old bullfighters' cafe, and drank coffee and then came back and wrote *Ten Indians*. This made me very sad and I drank some brandy and went to sleep. I'd forgotten to eat and one

of the waiters brought me up some bacalao and a small steak and fried potatoes and a bottle of Valdepenas.

The woman who ran the Pension was always worried that I did not eat enough and sent the waiter. I remember sitting up in bed and eating and drinking the Valdepenas. The waiter said he would bring up another bottle. He said the Senora wanted to know if I was going to write all night. I said no, I thought I would lay off for a while. Why don't you try to write just one more, the waiter said. I'm only supposed to write one, I said. Nonsense, he said. You could write six. I'll try tomorrow, I said.

The Three Day Blow

'Let's have another drink,' Nick said.

'I think there's another bottle open in the locker,' Bill said.

He kneeled down in the corner in front of the locker and brought out a square-faced bottle.

'It's Scotch,' he said.

'I'll get some more water,' Nick said. He went out into the kitchen again. He filled the pitcher with the dipper, dipping cold spring water from the pail. On his way back to the living-room he passed a mirror in the dining-room and looked in it. His face looked strange. He smiled at the face in the mirror and it grinned back at him. He winked at it and went on. It was not his face but it didn't make any difference.

Bill had poured out the drinks.

'That's an awfully big shot,' Nick said.

'Not for us, Wemedge,' Bill said.

'What'll we drink to?' Nick asked, holding up the glass.

'Let's drink to fishing,' Bill said.

'All right,' Nick said. 'Gentlemen, I give you fishing.'

'All fishing,' Bill said. 'Everywhere.'

'Fishing,' Nick said. 'That's what we drink to.'

'It's better than baseball,' Bill said.

'There isn't any comparison,' Nick said. 'How did we ever get talking about baseball?'

'It was a mistake,' Bill said. 'Baseball is a game for louts.'

They drank all that was in their glasses.

'Now let's drink to Chesterton.'

'And Walpole,' Nick interposed.

Nick poured out the liquor. Bill poured in the water. They looked at each other. They felt very fine.

Evelyn Waugh

Stories of drinking flood through the memories of all who knew of Evelyn Waugh and his generation, from youthful days of drunken indiscretion in the glittering 1920s to later but no less alcoholic years when the Bright Young Things had become older and a little tarnished.

Heavy drinking was a principal component of university life for Waugh and his contemporaries in the drinking set to which he belonged. He wrote to a friend that the art of drinking was the greatest thing Oxford had to teach. These were days of binges on beer, strong beer at eightpence a pint, and hazy evenings of dimly-remembered escapades. There were groups such as the Hypocrites' Club, where effeminate, if not homosexual, young men grew ever more affectionate and ever more drunken as the nights wore on. Some were rich, aristocratic, even brilliant and many became part of Waugh's life, emerging later in his books, especially in the pages of *Brideshead Revisited*.

The partying continued after university, in hectic 1920s London, with endless, sometimes distinctly louche parties followed by visits to fashionable clubs and then back home at six in the morning. A friend remembered him calling for her at four in the afternoon, armed with three bottles of champagne which were polished off before starting the evening's round of parties.

As with most novelists, his life spawned his art. Forays into schoolmastering and journalism contributed to delicious comedies such as *Decline and Fall* and *Scoop*. Later experiences in the war led to *Put Out More Flags* and the *Sword of Honour* trilogy.

After the war he returned to his country home to find 'a few dozen bottles in the cellar, Dow's '22 in fine condition' and rural life was enlivened by regular visits to London. The drinking continued unabated. His diary is a litany of drunken experiences. On 16 July, 1946, an entry reads: 'Tuesday, a drunken day; lunched at Beefsteak … Drinking in White's most of the afternoon. Then to Beefsteak where I got drunk with Kenneth Wagg and insulted R A Butler. Then to St James's for another bottle of champagne where I insulted Beverly Baxter ...'

The bright, waspish Waugh of the 1920s and 1930s metamorphosed with age into a baleful, boorish country gentleman who hated the modern world and grew into a crusty old snob. His rudeness became legendary: on meeting Cecil Beaton at a party he bellowed 'Here's someone who can tell us all about buggery!' With age he began to be concerned about the length of time he had to endure hangovers, and on what he considered to be merely light drinking.

In 1964 he wrote to a friend that he had practically given up drinking and had informed his doctor of his new sobriety in taking 'only about 7 bottles of wine and 3 of spirits a week.' 'A week? Surely you mean a month?' queried the doctor. 'No,' said Waugh, 'and I smoke 30 cigars a week and take 40 grains of sodium amytal.'

A lifetime of heavy drinking does not seem to have ruined his palate or affected his appreciation of wine. In his last years, gin was a constant companion but champagne was a favourite tipple. His advice on the ideal circumstances in which it should be drunk, which appeared in *Vogue* in 1965, is well worth heeding today:

'For two intimates, lovers or comrades, to spend a quiet evening with a magnum, drinking no aperitif, nothing but a glass of cognac after – that is the ideal . . .'

Brideshead Revisited

One day we went down to the cellars with Wilcox and saw the empty bays which had once held a vast store of wine; one transept only was used now; there the bins were well stocked, some of them with vintages fifty years old.

'There's been nothing added since his Lordship went abroad,' said Wilcox. 'A lot of the old wine wants drinking up. We ought to have laid down the eighteens and twenties. I've had several letters about it from the wine merchants, but her Ladyship says to ask Lord Brideshead, and he says to ask his Lordship, and his Lordship says to ask the lawyers. That's how we get low. There's enough here for ten years at the rate it's going, but how shall we be then?'

Wilcox welcomed our interest; we had bottles brought up

from every bin, and it was during those tranquil evenings with Sebastian that I first made a serious acquaintance with wine and sowed the seed of that rich harvest which was to be my stay in many barren years. We would sit, he and I, in the Painted Parlour with three bottles open on the table and three glasses before each of us; Sebastian had found a book on wine-tasting, and we followed its instructions in detail. We warmed the glass slightly at a candle, filled it a third high, swirled the wine round, nursed it in our hands, held it to the light, breathed it, sipped it, filled our mouths with it, and rolled it over the tongue, ringing it on the palate like a coin on a counter, tilted our heads back and let it trickle down the throat. Then we talked of it and nibbled Bath Oliver biscuits, and passed on to another wine; then back to the first, then on to another, until all three were in circulation and the order of glasses got confused, and we fell out over which was which, and we passed the glasses to and fro between us until there were six glasses, some of them with mixed wines in them which we had filled from the wrong bottle, till we were obliged to start again with three clean glasses each, and the bottles were empty and our praise of them wilder and more exotic.

'... It is a little, shy wine like a gazelle.'

'Like a leprechaun.'

'Dappled, in a tapestry meadow.'

'Like a flute by still water.'

'... And this is a wise old wine.'

'A prophet in a cave.'

'... And this is a necklace of pearls on a white neck.'

'Like a swan.'

'Like the last unicorn.'

And we would leave the golden candlelight of the dining-room for the starlight outside and sit on the edge of the fountain, cooling our hands in the water and listening drunkenly to its splash and gurgle over the rocks.

'Ought we to be drunk *every* night?' Sebastian asked one morning.

'Yes, I think so.'

'I think so too.'

James Boswell

James Boswell is best known as the devoted chronicler of the life of Doctor Johnson, very much in the shadow of – and often the butt of – a great, erudite, disputatious and often pompous man.

What makes Boswell such a good biographer is his candour; he does not allow respect for his subject to affect truthful observations of the doctor. The same candour is applied to descriptions of his own life in, for example, his *London Journal*. The picture that emerges is of a cheeky, chatty, lustful, drunken and dissipated but engaging figure.

Much of his journal describes his romantic but determined assaults on women and the later agonizing over his shameful behaviour. No woman was safe from his advances: from common prostitutes to serving maids, ladies of fashion to those of the court. But he is always honest about the success, or otherwise, of these amours. On Sunday, June 5, 1763, he records meeting a compliant lady after a night of drinking and sexual indulgence with more than one woman. Despite the lady's 'endearing amorous blandishments' he confessed sadly 'alas, my last night's rioting … had quite enervated me, and I had no tender inclinations'. The lady was understanding and observed, perhaps sadly, that it happened very commonly after drinking.

Boswell was thrilled and honoured to make the acquaintance of Doctor Johnson and records each meeting and conversational exchange with care. There were many social gatherings of this kind: 'We sat between till one and two and finishing a couple of bottles of port. I went home in high exultation.'

Port figured strongly in these meetings. In July 1763 at the Mitre:

> Mr Johnson said, 'We will not drink two bottles of port.' When one was drank, he called for another pint; and when we had got to the bottom of that, and I was distributing it equally,
>
> 'Come,' said he, 'you need not measure it so exactly.'
>
> 'Sir,' said I, 'it is done.'
>
> 'Well, Sir,' said he, 'are you satisfied? Or would you choose another?'
>
> 'Would you, Sir?' said I.
>
> 'Yes,' said he, 'I think I would. I think two bottles would seem to be the quantity for us.'

This exchange is a little puzzling as it appears more than two bottles were consumed, a mistake which may have been due to Boswell's indifferent arithmetic or the excellence of the port.

Sometime during the drinking of the second bottle Johnson was moved to take Boswell cordially by the hand and murmur, 'My dear Boswell! I do love you very much.'

Boswell was gratified by the compliment at the time but sounded rueful the following day: 'A bottle of thick English port is a very heavy and inflammatory dose. I felt it last time that I drank it for the several days, and this morning it was boiling in my veins.'

Some scholars argue that Boswell was less of a drinker than is generally supposed, but this argument is surely defied by the evidence. Boswell's own words amply convey his beliefs on the subject.

The Hypochondriack

> I do fairly acknowledge that I love Drinking; that I have a constitutional inclination to indulge in fermented liquors, and that if it were not for the restraints of reason and religion, I am afraid I should be as constant a votary of Bacchus as any man. . . . Drinking is in reality an occupation which employs a considerable portion of the time of many people; and to conduct it in the most rational and agreeable manner is one of the great arts of living.
>
> It is in vain for those who drink liberally to say that it is only for the sake of good company. Because it is very certain that if the wine were removed the company would soon break up, and it is plain that where wine is largely drunk there is less true social intercourse than in almost any other situation. Every one is intent upon the main object. His faculties are absorbed in the growing ebriety, the progress of which becomes more rapid every round, and all are for the moment persuaded of the force of that riotous maxim which I believe has been seriously uttered, that 'Conversation spoils drinking.'
>
> Where we so framed that it were possible by perpetual supplies of wine to keep ourselves for ever gay and happy, there could be no doubt that drinking would be the *summum bonum*, the chief good, to find out which philosophers have been so variously busied. We should then indeed produce in ourselves by the juice of the grape the effects which the seducing serpent pretended our

first parents would feel by eating of the forbidden tree in the midst of the garden. We should 'be as gods knowing good and evil;' and such a wild imagination of felicity must have filled the mind of Homer, when he thought of representing the gods of the Greeks as drinking in heaven, as he does in so high a strain of poetry, that one forgets the absurdity of the mythology. But we know from humiliating experience that men cannot be kept long in a state of elevated drunkenness.

English Inns

Who'er has travelled life's dull round,
Wher'er his stage may have been,
May sigh to think how oft he found
The warmest welcome – at an Inn.

William Shenstone

George Borrow

George Borrow is yet another of those Victorian writers, hugely popular in their day, who have been allowed to settle into dusty obscurity. His books are more often seen in cheap bargain boxes outside bookshops than on the shelves inside, which is a pity.

Borrow was a phenomenon, a self-taught polyglot able to speak some thirteen languages, not only the generally known languages of French, German and Russian but less well-known tongues such as Danish and Romany. He had a lifelong detestation of anything he regarded as genteel and was drawn to underprivileged and stigmatized groups, such as gypsies, whom he admired and joined in their roamings, as can be seen in *Lavengro* and *Romany Rye*.

Borrow was a big man – about 6 feet, 3 inches tall – and strong. He was not afraid to use this strength in physical confrontations, a quality sometimes called upon when travelling with gypsies in Britain or on the roads of Spain and Russia. His powerful physical presence was recalled by an observer at Ascot in 1872. A disagreement had broken out between a large gang of gypsies and two or three hundred soldiers from Windsor, and a major battle was imminent. Suddenly, 'an arbiter appeared, a white-haired, brown-eyed, calm Colossus, speaking Romany fluently, and drinking deep draughts of ale – in a quarter of an hour Tommy Atkins and Anselo Stanley were sworn friends over a loving quart.'

Inns and drinking are common themes of his ramblings around Britain. Beer, mead, even champagne, are drunk and there are opinions on the best drink of all, with old ale winning the verdict of *Romany Rye*.

For some reason, perhaps connected with Spain, Borrow had a violent dislike of sherry. When it is mentioned in his books, it is always critically. Edward Fitzgerald, translator of the *Rubaiyat of Omar Khayyam*, was Borrow's neighbour and remembered a visit by him when the sore subject of sherry cropped up. Borrow was drinking strong port and, although Fitzgerald was drinking sherry, Borrow 'expressed contempt for anyone who could drink sherry'.

Although not a particularly devout Christian, Borrow's travels to Spain and Russia were funded by the British Bible Society, for whom he worked as a translator and distributor of bibles. The society's aim was to spread the knowledge of the gospel to less fortunate races by distributing translations of the Bible in many languages – twenty versions were distributed in Asia in the nineteenth century.

From these Spanish experiences came Borrow's *The Bible in Spain*, the book that first brought him success. Far from being a pious work describing sober missionary work, it is a rollicking account of his travels and adventures, of meeting desperate banditti in a remote inn where they: 'are in the habit of coming and spending their money, the fruits of their criminal daring; there they dance and sing, eat fricasseed rabbits and olives, and drink the muddy but strong wine of the Alemtejo.'

His chosen companion, he says, 'is inordinately given to drink, and of so quarrelsome a disposition that he is almost constantly involved in some broil.' Borrow himself was not above such 'broils', especially when clashing with authority.

In Borrow's later years as a highly successful author he became a rather forbidding figure, but a friend recalled that 'no man was more hearty than he over a glass'. He seemed a fortunate man, hale and hearty in late life, still proud of his physical strength, swimming in the sea off the Norfolk coast summer and winter until he was about 70. But there was a sadness in him, as he revealed in *Romany Rye* when looking back on his wanderings in Britain:

> On the whole, I journeyed along very pleasantly, certainly quite as pleasantly as I do at present, now that I am become a gentleman and weigh sixteen stone, though some people would say that my present manner of travelling is much the most preferable, riding as I now do, instead of leading my horse; receiving the homage of ostlers instead of their familiar nods; sitting down to dinner in the parlour of the best inn I can find, instead of passing the brightest part of the day in the kitchen of the village ale-house; carrying on my argument after dinner on the subject of the corn-laws, with the best commercial gentlemen on the road, instead of being glad, whilst sipping a pint of beer, to get into conversation with blind trampers or maimed Abraham sailors, regaling themselves on half-pints at the said village hostelries. Many people will doubtless say that things have altered wonderfully with me for the better, and they would be right, provided I possessed now what I then carried about with me on my journeys – the spirit of youth. Youth is the only season for enjoyment, and the first twentyfive years of one's life are worth all the rest of the longest life of man.

The Romany Rye

The inn, of which I had become an inhabitant, was a place of infinite life and bustle. Travellers of all descriptions, from all the cardinal points, were continually stopping at it; and to attend to their wants, and minister to their convenience, an army of servants, of one description or other, was kept; waiters, chambermaids, grooms, postillions, shoe-blacks, cooks, scullions, and what not, for there was a barber and hair-dresser, who had been at Paris, and talked French with a cockney accent; the French sounding all the better, as no accent is so melodious as the cockney. Jacks creaked in the kitchens turning round spits, on which large joints of meat piped and smoked before the great big fires. There was running up and down stairs, and along galleries, slamming of doors, cries of 'Coming, sir,' and 'Please to step this way, ma'am,' during eighteen hours of the four-and-twenty. Truly a very great place for life and bustle was this inn. And often in after life, when lonely and melancholy, I have called up the time I spent there, and never failed to become cheerful from the recollection.

I found the master of the house a very kind and civil person. Before being an inn-keeper he had been in some other line of business, but on the death of the former proprietor of the inn had married his widow, who was still alive, but being somewhat infirm, lived in a retired part of the house. I have said that he was kind and civil; he was, however, not one of those people who suffer themselves to be made fools of by anybody; he knew his customers, and had a calm clear eye, which would look through a man without seeming to do so. The accommodation of his house was of the very best description; his wines were good, his viands equally so, and his charges not immoderate; though he very properly took care of himself. He was no vulgar inn-keeper, had a host of friends, and deserved them all. During the time I lived with him, he was presented, by a large assemblage of his friends and customers, with a dinner at his own house, which was very costly, and at which the best of wines were sported, and after the dinner with a piece of plate, estimated at fifty guineas. He received the plate, made a neat speech of thanks, and when the bill was called for, made another neat speech, in which he refused to receive one farthing for the entertainment, ordering in at the same time two dozen more of the best champagne and sitting down amidst uproarious applause, and cries of 'You shall be no loser by it!' Nothing very wonderful in such conduct, some people will say; I don't say there is, nor have I any intention to endeavour to persuade the reader that the landlord was a Carlo Borromeo; he merely gave a quid pro quo; but it is not every person who will give you a quid pro quo. Had he been a vulgar publican, he would have sent in a swinging bill after receiving the plate; 'but then no vulgar publican would have been presented with plate;' perhaps not, but many a vulgar public character has been presented with plate, whose admirers never received a quid pro quo, except in the shape of a swinging bill.

I found my duties of distributing hay and corn, and keeping an account thereof, anything but disagreeable, particularly after I had acquired the good-will of the old ostler, who at first looked upon me with rather an evil eye, considering me somewhat in the light of one who had usurped an office which belonged to himself by the right of succession; but there was little gall in the old fellow, and by speaking kindly to him, never giving myself any airs of assumption, but, above all, by frequently reading the newspapers to him – for, though passionately fond of news and politics, he was unable to read – I soon succeeded in placing myself on excellent terms with him. A regular character was that old ostler, he was a Yorkshireman by birth, but had seen a great deal of life in the vicinity of London, to which, on the death of his parents, who were very poor people, he went at a very early age. Amongst other places where he had served as ostler was a small inn at Hounslow, much frequented by highwaymen, whose exploits he was fond of narrating.

George Crabbe

George Crabbe is inextricably linked in the modern mind with the gloomy tale of tragic Peter Grimes, who is best known as the eponymous hero of Benjamin Britten's opera.

If anyone thinks of the original author, Crabbe, at all, he is probably imagined as a dark, brooding figure in the mould of Grimes. By all accounts, he was nothing like this but was noted for amiability and charm. His son described his character thus: 'The chief characteristic of his heart was benevolence, so that his mind was a buoyant exuberance of thought and perpetual exercise of intellect.' He was quite a figure in his day: an admired poet, praised by Dr Johnson, enjoying the patronage of Edmund Burke. His personality was immediately attractive, as one observer grunted irritably: 'Damme, Sir, the very first time Crabbe dined at my house, he made love to my sister.'

Born in Suffolk at Aldeburgh, he was a parson-poet, spending the major part of his life as a country cleric. Although a man of the cloth, Crabbe wrote a great deal about inns and, indeed, of drink, descriptions which can only have come from personal observation and experience. We know, however, that his preferred stimulant was a regular dose of opium, such addiction being unremarkable in his day. However, his poetry, especially the account of life in his poem, 'The Borough', suggests a familiarity with the more common stimulants of the period.

In the 'Tavern' he paid tribute to the role of the pub:

All the comforts of life in a Tavern are known
'Tis his home who possesses not one of his Own.

The tavern was the setting, too, for the anguish of Peter Grimes:

On an oak settle, in his maudlin grief
This he revolved, and drunk for his relief.

There is a clear ring of authenticity in his account of the pubs of the community as he takes the reader on a guided tour, or pub crawl, of them. There are a great many of them: the Lion, the Bear and Crown, Queen Caroline, Fountain, Vine; and others – including his favourite, the Queen, which is described below.

The Borough

There fires inviting blazed, and all around
Was heard the tinkling bells' seducing sound;
The nimble waiters to that sound from far
Sprang to the call, then hasten'd to the bar;
Where a glad priestess of the temple sway'd,
The most obedient, and the most obeyed;

Rosy and round, adorn'd in crimson vest,
And flaming ribbons at her ample breast: –
She, skilled like Circe, tried her guests to move,
With looks of welcome and with words of love;
And such her potent charms, that men unwise
Were soon transformed and fitted for the sties.
Her port in bottles stood, a well-stain'd row,
Drawn for the evening from the pipe below;
Three powerful spirits fill'd a parted case,
Some cordial bottles stood in secret place;
Her plate was splendid, and her glasses clean;
Basins and bowls were ready on the stand,
And measures clatter'd in her powerful hand.

Crabbe has a little amusement at the activities of a Book Club which seems a little less than literary.

But our attractions are a stronger sort,
The earliest dainties and the oldest port,
All enter then with glee in every look,
And not a member thinks about a book.
There was no pause – the wine went quickly round,
Till struggling Fancy was by Bacchus bound;
Wine is to wit as water thrown on fire,
By duly sprinkling both are raised the higher;
This largely dealt, the vivid blaze they choke,
And all the genial flame goes off in smoke.
But when wine no more o'erwhelms the labouring brain,
But swerves a gentle stimulus; we know
How wit must sparkle, and how fancy flow.

Oliver Goldsmith

Modern writers find it mysterious – not to say irritating – that so many writers of the past managed to combine a vigorous social life and, at the same time, produce a substantial body of work. Oliver Goldsmith is typical: journalist, essayist, novelist, poet, playwright and one of the leading lights of eighteenth-century literary London. According to a contemporary he worked in the morning and 'spent the day generally convivially' and took his work with him when he retired for the night.

Goldsmith had a healthy appreciation of drink, writing in *She Stoops to Conquer*:

> Let schoolmasters puzzle their brain
> With grammar, and nonsense and learning.
> Good liquor, I stoutly maintain,
> Gives genius a better discerning.

His drinking apprenticeship was served in a fine school, Trinity College, Dublin, and he was the life and soul of the party (he was a skilled flute player) in Irish country houses. London provided many similar opportunities for a sociable soul. As a member of the literary circle that gathered around Dr Johnson there were hard-drinking literary dinners and improving conversation, as well as less cerebral occasions and uproarious boozing in Fleet Street pubs such as the Globe Tavern.

Sometimes he would seek quieter surroundings in which to work, such as the then village of Edgware. Even here, however, there was time for merriment because he and a friend, Edward Bott, would take the gig to town for dinner, returning late and in lively form. On one such journey Bott managed to hit a signpost but stubbornly insisted he was in the middle of the highway (yet another instance of apparently stationary objects mysteriously moving into the path of those who have taken drink).

Goldsmith must have cut an odd figure in society. He was stocky with a pockmarked face, an unusually large head and a strong Irish accent. Despite these disadvantages – or perhaps because of them – he loved to deck himself out in finery. He was always short of money, partly because he was extravagantly generous, but he never spared expense when it came to buying clothes. In 1767 he acquired a 'superfine frock-suit' and in 1768 his wardrobe was enhanced by a 'Tyrian bloom satin grain' suit and 'blue silk breeches'. It was probably a mistake to wear a new 'bloom-coloured' coat of which Goldsmith was very proud to a dinner party in the company of that notoriously slovenly dresser, Samuel Johnson. Goldsmith boasted that the tailor had begged him to mention his name as the maker of the coat. Johnson snorted, 'Why, Sir, that was because he knew the colour would attract crowds to gaze at it, and thus they might hear of him, and see how well he could make a coat even of so absurd a colour.'

Poor Goldsmith, as he was often referred to even by friends, was often the butt of company. It was David Garrick who wrote the mock epitaph:

> Here lies Nolly Goldsmith, for shortness call'd Noll,
> Who wrote like an angel, but talk'd like poor Poll.

Goldsmith returned the compliment a little later with:

> On the stage he was natural, simple, affecting,
> 'Twas only that, when he was off, he was acting.

Reverie at the Boar's Head Tavern in Eastcheap

'My dear Mrs Quickly,' cried I (for I knew her perfectly well at first sight). 'I am heartily glad to see you. How have you left Falstaff, Pistol and the rest of our friends below stairs? Brave and hearty, I hope?' In good sooth, replied she, he did deserve to live for ever; but he maketh foul work on't where he hath flitted. Queen Proserpine and he have quarrelled for his attempting a rape upon her divinity; and were it not that she still had bowels of compassion, it more than seems probable he might have been now sprawling in Tartarus.

I now found that spirits still preserve the frailties of the flesh; and that, according to the laws of criticism and dreaming, ghosts have been known to be guilty of even more than platonic affection; wherefore, as I found her too much moved on such a topic to proceed, I was resolved to change the subject, and, desiring she would pledge me in a bumper, observed with a sigh, that our sack was nothing now to what it was in former days: 'Ah Mrs Quickly, those were merry times when you drew sack for Prince Henry; men were twice as strong, and twice as wise, and much braver, and ten thousand times more charitable, than now. Those were the times! The battle of Agincourt was a victory indeed! Ever since that we have only been degenerating; and I have lived to see the day when drinking is no longer fashionable; when men wear clean shirts and women shew their necks and arms; all are degenerated, Mrs Quickly; and we shall probably, in another century, be frittered away into beaux or monkeys. Had you been on earth to see what I have seen, it would congeal all the blood in your body (your soul, I mean). Why our very nobility now have the intolerable arrogance, in spite of what is every day remonstrated from the press; our very nobility, I say, have the assurance of frequent assemblies and presume to be as merry as the vulgar. See, my very friends have scarcely manhood enough to sit to it till eleven; and I only am left to make a night on't. Pr'ythee do me the favour to console me a little for their absence by the story of your own adventure, or the history of the tavern where we are now sitting; I fancy the narrative may have something singular.'

... The story of my own adventures, replied the vision, is but short and unsatisfactory; for believe me, Mr Rigmarole, believe me, a woman with a butt of sack at her elbow, is never long-lived. Sir John's death afflicted me to such a degree, that I sincerely believe, to drown sorrow, I drank more liquor myself than I drew for my customers: my grief was sincere, and the sack was excellent. The prior of a neighbouring convent (for our priors then had as much power as a Middlesex justice now) he, I say, it was who gave me a licence for keeping a disorderly house; upon conditions I should never make hard bargains with the clergy, that he should have a bottle of sack every morning, and the liberty of confessing which of my girls he thought proper in private every night. I had continued for several years to pay this tribute; and he, it must be confessed, continued as rigorously to act it. I grew old insensibly; my customers continued, however, to compliment my looks while I was by, but I could hear them say I was wearing when my back was turned. The prior however still was constant, and so were half his convent: but one fatal morning he missed the usual beverage; for I had incautiously drank over-night the last bottle myself. What will you have on't – The very next day Doll Tearsheet and I were sent to the house of correction, and accused of keeping a low bawdy-house. In short, we were so well purified there with stripes, mortification, and penance, that we were afterwards utterly unfit for worldly conversation: though sack would have killed me, had I stuck to it; yet I soon died for want of a drop of something comfortable, and fairly left my body to the care of the beadle.

Samuel Johnson

Dr Johnson seems to have pronounced more on the subject of drink than anyone in history, but this is an illusion. The truth is that he pronounced more on everything than anyone else. He had opinions on all things; pretty well any subject could draw a witty, learned or barbed apophthegm.

With the invaluable help of Boswell he has become a kind of patron saint of drinkers, because he not only spoke often of drink but spent much of his time drinking. Taverns were his home, dining out his rule. When he went to a tavern he was often among the last to leave.

Johnson had his own peculiar timetable, generally leaving his home at four in the afternoon and returning at about two in the morning. Boswell recalled meeting him in Fleet Street at one in the morning in the early days of their acquaintanceship. The young admirer suggested they visit the Mitre but the experienced Johnson refused: 'Sir, it is too late. They won't let us in.'

Johnson did not allow the dignity of his reputation to interfere with his social pleasures. One night two young friends staggered out of a tavern at three in the morning and knocked loudly at Johnson's door. He appeared at the window in his nightshirt and wig with a poker in his hand but when they called him to come out for a drink he responded gaily: 'What, is it you, you dogs! I'll have frisk with you!' He was soon dressed and went with them to a Covent Garden tavern where they supped on Bishop (a mulled port), a drink Johnson particularly liked.

Boswell speculated about when the doctor did his literary work as he spent most of the day in conversation and seldom refused an invitation to a tavern. When ill-health demanded that he should moderate his drinking, Johnson found abstinence easier than moderation and, indeed, abstained for quite long periods in his life.

Port was his staple drink: a thick, powerful potion in the eighteenth century. He was well able to take a bottle or so at a sitting and claimed, 'I have drunk three bottles of port without being the worse for it.' It does not seem to have impaired his wits. For example, on the question of a man speaking the truth when having taken enough wine, *in vino veritas*: 'I would not keep company with a fellow, who lyes as long as he is sober, and whom you must make drunk before you can get a word of truth out of him.'

He could be sharp or even downright rude. Discussing one evening the agreeable subject of drinking, a gentleman said: 'You know, Sir, drinking drives away care and makes us forget whatever is disagreeable. Would you not allow a man to drink for that reason?'

'Yes, Sir, if he sat next you,' was Johnson's crushing response.

Inevitably, it is Boswell who records a story that illustrates why Johnson is so widely quoted on drink:

> He asserted that the present was never a happy state to any human being; but that, as every part of life, of which we are conscious, was at some point of time a period yet to come, in which felicity was expected, there was some happiness produced by hope. Being pressed upon this subject, and asked if he really was of opinion that though, in general, happiness was very rare in human life, a man was not sometimes happy the moment that was present, he answered, 'Never, but when he is drunk.'

Boswell's Life of Johnson

There is no private house in which people can enjoy themselves so well, as at a capital tavern. Let there be ever so great plenty of good things, ever so much grandeur, ever so much elegance, ever so much desire that every body should be easy: in the nature of things it cannot be: there must always be some degree of care and anxiety. The master of the house is anxious to entertain his guests; the guests are anxious to be agreeable to him: and no man, but a very impudent dog indeed, can as freely command what is in another man's house, as if it were his own. Whereas, at a tavern there is a general freedom from anxiety. You are sure you are welcome: and the more noise you make, the more trouble you give, the more good things you call for, the welcomer you are. No servants will attend you with the alacrity which waiters do, who are incited by the prospect of an immediate reward in proportion as they please. No, Sir; there is nothing which has yet been contrived by man, by which so much happiness is produced as by a good tavern or inn.

On Wednesday April 7, I dined with him at Sir Joshua Reynolds'. I have not marked what company was there. Johnson harangued upon the qualities of different liquors; and spoke with great contempt of claret, as so weak, that 'a man would be drowned by it before it made him drunk.' He was persuaded to drink one glass of it, that he might judge, not from recollection, which might be dim, but from immediate sensation. He shook his head, and said, 'Poor stuff! No, Sir, claret is the liquor for boys; port for men; but he who aspires to be a hero (smiling) must drink brandy. In the first place, the flavour of brandy is most grateful to the palate; and then brandy will do soonest for a man what drinking *can* do for him. There are, indeed, few who are able to drink brandy. That is a power rather to be wished for than attained. And yet, (proceeded he) as in all pleasure hope is a considerable part, I know not but fruition is wine only to the eye; it is wine neither while you are drinking it, nor after you have drunk it; it neither pleases the taste, nor exhilarates the spirits.' I reminded him how heartily he and I used to drink wine together, when we were first acquainted; and how I used to have a head-ache after sitting up with him. He did not like to have this recalled, or, perhaps, thinking that I boasted improperly, resolved to have a witty stroke at me: 'Nay, Sir, it was not the *wine* that made your head ache, but the *sense* that I put into it.' BOSWELL: 'What, Sir! will sense make the head ache?' JOHNSON: 'Yes, Sir, (with a smile) when it is not used to it.'

Talking of the effects of drinking, he said, 'Drinking may be practised with great prudence; a man who exposes himself when he is intoxicated, has not the art of getting drunk; a sober man who happens occasionally to get drunk, readily enough goes into a new company, which a man who has been drinking should never do. Such a man will undertake any thing; he is without skill in inebriation. I used to slink home, when I had drunk too much. A man accustomed to self-examination will be conscious when he is drunk, though an habitual drunkard will not be conscious of it. I knew a physician who for forty years was not sober; yet in a pamphlet, which he wrote upon fevers, he appealed to Garrick and me for his vindication from a charge of drunkenness. A bookseller (naming him) who got a large fortune by trade, was so habitually and equably drunk that his most intimate friends never perceived that he was more sober at one time than another.'

Ben Jonson

Ben Jonson was the sort of man who could easily have strutted from the pages of one of his own plays: brilliant, argumentative, truculent, especially when in drink. He was a mighty drinker, by all accounts, and his plays present a vivid picture of the Elizabethan tavern and the parade of characters who could be found there. A contemporary described him as: 'a great lover and praiser of himself, a condemner and scorner of others, given rather to lose a friend than a jest, jealous of every word and action of those about him, especially after drink.' A dangerous, violent drinker, Jonson once escaped death when killing a fellow actor in a brawl.

His friends included Shakespeare, Donne, Bacon, Fletcher and Herrick – Shakespeare was in the cast of his *Every Man in His Humour*, performed at the Globe in 1598. Another acquaintance, Izaak Walton, said: 'He would many times exceed in drinke (Canarie was his beloved liquor), then he would tumble home to bed, and, when he had thoroughly perspired, then to studie.' Walton recorded that he had many pensions, from the City, the King, the nobility and the gentry, 'which was well payd for love or fere of his raling in verse or prose or boeth'.

In his last years – again, according to Walton – he lived with a woman and 'neither he nor she tooke much care for the next weeke; and would be sure not to want wine; of which he usually tooke too much before he went to bed, if not oftener or soner.' According to Jonson's own testimony, good wine sparkled his imagination: 'I laid the plot of my *Volpone* and wrote most of it after a present of ten dozen of palm sack from my very good Lord T—'. In another note he wrote, 'The first speech in my *Cataline*, spoken by Sylla's ghost, was writ after I parted with my friends at the Devil's Tavern; I had drunk well that night, and had brave notions. There is one scene in that play which I think is flat – I resolve to drink no more water in my wine.'

John Aubrey did not know Jonson, of course, but had information from Izaak Walton and wrote about Jonson in his *Brief Lives*:

A grace by B Jonson before King James:

Our King and Queen the Lord-God blesse,
The Paltzgrave and the Lady Besse.
And God blesse every living thing

Ben Jonson

That lives, and breathes, and loves the King.
God Blesse the Councell of Estate,
And Buckingham the Fortunate,
God Blesse them all, and keep them safe:
And God blesse me, and God blesse Ralph.

The king was mighty curious to know who this Ralph was and Ben Jonson told him he was the drawer at the Swanne Taverne by Charing-Crosse, who drew him good Canarie. For this Drollerie his Majestie gave him an hundred pounds.

Bartholomew Fair

The Pig Woman

URSULA Fie upon't! Who would wear out their youth and prime thus in roasting of pigs, that had any cooler vocation? Hell's a kind of cold cellar to't, a very fine vault, o'my conscience! What Mooncalf!

MOONCALF (*within*) Here, Mistress.

NIGHTINGALE How, now, Urs'la? In a heat, in a heat?

URSULA (*to* MOONCALF) My chair, you false faucet you; and my morning's draught, quickly, a bottle of ale to quench me, rascal, – I am all fire and fat, Nightingale; I shall e'en melt away to the first woman, a rib again, I am afraid. I do water the ground in knots as I go, like a great garden-pot; you may follow me by the S's I make.

NIGHTINGALE Alas, good Urs; was 'Zekiel here this morning?

URSULA 'Zekiel? What 'Zekiel?

NIGHTINGALE 'Zekiel Edgworth, the civil cutpurse; you know him well enough – he talks bawdy to you still. I call him my secretary.

URSULA He promised to be here this morning, I remember.

NIGHTINGALE When he comes, bid him stay. I'll be back again presently.

URSULA Best take your morning's dew in your belly, Nightingale. (MOONCALF *brings in the chair.*) Come sir, set it here. Did not I bid you should get this chair let out o'the sides for me, that my hips might play? You'll never think of anything till your dame be rump-galled. 'Tis well, changeling; because it can take in your grasshopper's thighs, you care for no more. Now you look as you had been i' the corner o'the booth, fleaing your breech with a candle's end, and set fire o'the Fair. Fill, stot, fill.

OVERDO (*aside*) This pig-woman do I know, and I will put her in for my second enormity. She hath been before me, punk, pinnace, and bawd, any time these two and twenty years, upon record i' the Pie-powders.

URSULA Fill again, you unlucky vermin.

MOONCALF Pray you be not angry, mistress; I'll ha' it widened anon.

URSULA No, no, I shall e'en dwindle away to't, ere the Fair be done, you think, now you ha' heated me! A poor vexed thing I am. I feel myself dropping already, as fast as I can; two stone o'suet a day is my proportion. I can but hold life and soul together with this (here's to you, Nightingale) and a whiff of tobacco, at most. Where's my pipe now? Not filled? Thou arrant incubee!

NIGHTINGALE Nay, Urs'la, thou'lt gall between the tongue and the teeth with freeting, now.

URSULA How can I hope that ever he'll discharge his place of trust – tapster, man of reckoning under me – that remembers nothing I say to him? (*Exit* NIGHTINGALE.) But look to't, sirrah, you were best; threepence a pipeful I will ha'made of all my whole half-pound of tobacco, and a quarter of a pound of colts-foot mixed with it too, to eke it out. I that have dealt so long in the fire will not be to seek in smoke, now. Then, six and twenty shillings a barrel I will advance o'my beer, and fifty shillings a hundred o' my bottle-ale; I ha' told you the ways how to raise it. Froth your cans well i' the filling, at length, rogue, and jog your bottle o' the buttock, sirrah, then skink out the first glass, ever, and drink with all companies, though you be sure to be drunk; you misreckon the better, and be less ashamed on't. But your true trick rascal, must be ever busy, and mis-take away the bottles and cans in haste before they be half drunk off, and never hear anybody call (if they should chance to mark you) till you ha' brought fresh, and be able to forswear 'em. Give me a drink of ale.

Alfred, Lord Tennyson

The popular impression of Alfred, Lord Tennyson is of someone stately, statuesque, monumental. To modern eyes he is, perhaps, the literary equivalent of a magnificent Victorian tombstone in marble.

But there was another Tennyson: a large, romantic singer of songs, a lover of late nights and strong drink, especially port. After convivial sessions in London pubs and restaurants he would march the streets, a tall, bony, wild-haired figure, declaiming poetic lines to the night air.

The recollections of his friends are full of references to long evenings of smoking and drinking and parting at two, three and four in the morning. Edward Fitzgerald, the translator of the *Rubaiyat of Omar Khayyam*, wrote of a typical visit in 1838.

> We have had Alfred Tennyson here, very droll, and very wayward; and much sitting up nights till two or three in the morning with pipes in our mouths: at which good hour we would get Alfred to give us some of his magic music, which he does between growling and smoking, and so to bed.

Fitzgerald described his voice like 'the sound of a far sea or of a pine wood'.

Discovering Tennyson had a sense of humour is slightly shocking, as if learning Queen Victoria had a taste for boozy ballads. After one of his regular jaunts, he and a group of friends piled into a horse-bus and the conductor gave his regular shout of 'Are you full inside?' To which the future poet laureate answered, 'Yes, the last glass did for me.'

For virtually all of his life he drank at least a bottle of port at dinner, but it seems he was sometimes forgetful about sharing the bottle. Peter Levi, in his biography of the poet, tells of a visit by the actor Henry Irving. When the first bottle arrived Tennyson poured a glass for Irving and drank the rest himself. Another bottle was ordered and he again gave Irving a single glass, drinking the remainder himself. The next day he looked at Irving thoughtfully and asked, 'Tell me, is it your custom always to consume two entire bottles of port every evening?'

Illness in his middle years led to interruption of the port habit when his doctors advised sherry as an acceptable alternative, a suggestion with which he complied; indeed, he became a knowledgeable and discriminating judge of sherry. When the period of comparative abstinence was over he returned to fine port, praising in verse port which calmed rather than inflamed: 'His richest beeswing from a bin reserved/For banquets.'

Despite everything, drinking too much, incessant smoking – 'the strongest and most stinking tobacco out of a small, blackened pipe on an average nine hours a day' reported a friend – he lived to the ripe old age of 83. He faced his end with equanimity; one of his few grumbles was on having to drink whisky instead of port, and he passed away peacefully on 6 October 1892.

Will Waterproof's Lyrical Monologue

O plump head-waiter at The Cock,
   To which I most resort,
How goes the time? 'Tis five o'clock.
   Go fetch a pint of port:
But let it not be such as that
   You set before chance-comers,
But such whose father-grape grew fat
   On Lusitanian summers.
No vain libation to the Muse,
   But may she still be kind,
And whisper lovely words, and use
   Her influence on the mind,
To make me write my random rhymes,
   Ere they be half-forgotten;
Nor add and alter, many times,
   Till all be ripe and rotten.

I pledge her, and she comes and dips
   Her laurel in the wine,
And lays it thrice upon my lips,
   These favoured lips of mine;
Until the charm have power to make
   New lifeblood warm the bosom,
And barren commonplaces break
   In full and kindly blossom.

I pledge her silent at the board;
   Her gradual fingers steal

And touch upon the master-chord
  Of all I felt and feel.
Old wishes, ghosts of broken plans,
  And phantom hopes assemble;
And that child's heart within the man's
  Begins to move and tremble.

Through many an hour of summer suns,
  By many pleasant ways,
Against its fountain upward runs
  The current of my days:
I kiss the lips I once have kissed;
  The gas-light wavers dimmer;
And softly, through a vinous mist,
  My college friendships glimmer.

Head-water, honoured by the guest
  Half-mused, or reeling ripe,
The pint, you brought me, was the best
  That ever came from pipe.
But though the port surpasses praise,
  My nerves have dealt with stiffer.
Is there some magic in the place?
  Or do my peptics differ?

For since I came to live and learn,
  No pint of white or red
Had ever half the power to turn
  This wheel within my head,
Which bears a seasoned brain about,
  Unsubject to confusion,
Though soaked and saturate, out and out,
  Through every convolution.

For I am of a numerous house,
  With many kinsmen gay,
Where long and largely we carouse
  As who shall say me nay;
Each month, a birth-day coming on,
  We drink defying trouble,
Or sometimes two would meet in one,
  And then we drank it double;

Whether the vintage, yet unkept,
   Had relish fiery-new,
Or elbow-deep in sawdust, slept,
   As old as Waterloo;
Or stowed, when classic Canning died,
   Its musty bins and chambers,
Had cast upon its crusty side
   The gloom of ten Decembers.

The Muse, the jolly Muse, it is!
   She answered to my call,
She changes with that mood or this,
   Is all-in-all to all:
She lit the spark within my throat,
   To make my blood run quicker,
Used all her fiery will, and smote
   Her life into the liquor.

J R R Tolkien

Fantastic as Tolkien's *Lord of the Rings* is, there are elements of reality – not least in the hobbits' enjoyment of good beer. There is nothing uproarious or wild in their drinking, simply a quiet appreciation – which was very much the way Tolkien and his friends enjoyed their ale.

Tolkien the author was also, of course, J R R Tolkien, Oxford don and specialist in Anglo-Saxon and English. He was a member of an informal literary society, the Inklings, with other brilliant university men such as C S Lewis, author of the *Screwtape Letters* and much more. Tolkien explained that the name was a pun 'suggesting people with vague or half-formed intimations and ideas plus those who dabble in ink'.

A favourite meeting place was the Eagle and Child pub in Oxford – known locally as the Bird and Baby. In a small back room the members would down pints of beer or cider (one of the attractions of the pub was its powerful draught cider, known as 'Bung Misery') while discoursing on matters literary and theological.

The group, individually and collectively, used several Oxford watering holes – the Eastgate, the Mitre and so on – for pints and high-minded disputation. The great men relaxed occasionally with puns and bawdy stories but eavesdroppers had to have a reasonable command of Anglo-Saxon and Icelandic to be able to appreciate them. Tolkien (Tollers as he was known to his intimates) was well known for his spicy jests in Icelandic and was said to be able to produce bawdy stories in several languages.

The meetings were also held in college. Tolkien wrote of meeting a friend at the Mitre 'to take fuel on board before joining the well-oiled diners in Magdalen'. He greatly enjoyed the friendship of colleagues, writing of one: 'Your laugh in my heart echoes, when with you I quaff the pint that goes down quicker than a half because you're near.'

Beer played a significant part in the social life of the scholarly members of the Inklings. During the Second World War beer was scarce and the Bird and Baby often had a gloomy 'No Beer' sign on the door. One of the members said his idea of a good life would be to buy a pub, put up a No Beer sign, keep the customers out and 'drink the lot myself'.

The discernment brought to fine points of theology or philosophy was shown in assessments of beer, lesser brews being dismissed as 'varnish'. The quality of drink available was also a major consideration on walking holidays. Tolkien reported on a walk in the Malvern Hills, 'Only one really good inn, The Unicorn, which is all that you could desire in looks and otherwise. The Hertfordshire cider is astringent and thirst quenching.'

When the war ended the Inklings had decided how the victory was to be celebrated; according to Tolkien, 'to take a whole inn in the countryside for at least a week and spend it entirely on beer and talk'.

The Lord of the Rings

> Even from the outside the inn looked a pleasant house to familiar eyes. It had a front on the Road, and two wings running back on land partly cut out of the lower slopes of the hill, so that at the rear the second-floor windows were level with the ground. There was a wide arch leading to a courtyard between the two wings, and on the left under the arch there was a large doorway reached by a few broad steps. The door was open and light streamed out of it. Above the arch there was a lamp, and beneath it swung a

large signboard: a fat white pony reared up on its hind legs. Over the door was painted in white letters: THE PRANCING PONY by BARLIMAN BUTTERBUR. Many of the lower windows showed lights behind thick curtains.

As they hesitated outside in the gloom, someone began singing a merry song inside, and many cheerful voices joined loudly in the chorus. They listened to this encouraging sound for a moment and then got off their ponies. The song ended and there was a burst of laughter and clapping.

They led their ponies under the arch, and leaving them standing in the yard they climbed up the steps. Frodo went forward and nearly bumped into a short fat man with a bald head and a red face. He had a white apron on, and was bustling out of one door and in through another, carrying a tray laden with full mugs.

... He led them a short way down a passage, and opened a door. 'Here is a nice little parlour!' he said. 'I hope it will suit. Excuse me now, I'm that busy. No time for talking. I must be trotting. It's hard work for two legs, but I don't get thinner. I'll look in again later. If you want anything, ring the hand-bell, and Nob will come. If he don't come, ring and shout!'

Off he went at last, and left them feeling rather breathless. He seemed capable of an endless stream of talk, however busy he might be. They found themselves in a small and cosy room. There was a bit of bright fire burning on the hearth, and in front of it were some low and comfortable chairs. There was a round table, already spread with a white cloth, and on it was a large hand-bell. But Nob, the hobbit servant, came bustling in long before they thought of ringing. He brought candles and a tray full of plates.

'Will you be wanting anything to drink, masters?' he asked. 'And shall I show you the bedrooms, while your supper is got ready?'

They were washed and in the middle of good deep mugs of beer when Mr Butterbur and Nob came in again. In a twinkling the table was laid. There was hot soup, cold meats, a blackberry tart, new loaves, slabs of butter, and half a ripe cheese: good plain food, as good as the Shire could show, and homelike enough to dispel the last of Sam's misgivings (already much relieved by the excellence of the beer).

DISCOURSE OF DRINKERS

Among foaming bottles and ale-washed wits.

William Shakespeare

I'll have another
Brendan Behan

Brendan Behan

Brendan Behan has become something of a mythic figure in the folklore of Irish drinking; a gargantuan drinker, a bold spirit, a roaring boy, matchless with the pint and the pun.

Unusually in matters Irish, there is no exaggeration in this portrait; he was one of the leading players on the Irish literary and drinking scene, which is often one and the same thing.

He was a Dubliner, a devoted patron of that city's many fine pubs. As Hemingway and others used the bars of Paris for writing, so did Behan the watering holes of Dublin, setting up his portable typewriter, with cigarette smoking and glass to hand, at McDaid's in Harry Street. At other times, the typewriter was ignored and he became the person best known to Dublin – the laughing, pugnacious, roisterer.

A frank and loving account of him is by J P Donleavy, who knew him well, supped with him, argued with him and scrapped with him. In Donleavy's hilarious *The History of the Ginger Man* he describes their amazing 'hooleys': drunken progressions through the bars of Dublin, talking – always talking – laughing, singing and – almost always – fighting, with each other if there was no one else available. There was even more to him than drinking and writing, says Donleavy. He was a brilliant mimic and had the ability to quote arcane British legal judgements from memory, no doubt to the astonishment of his pub audience.

His Dublin wit was famous. He it was who answered immigration authorities in Canada as to the purpose of his visit with the ringing declaration: 'To drink Canada Dry.'

He was an outrageous, demonic force. When in the West of Ireland he always made a pilgrimage to the local pub, followed by a visit to the local bookshop. He was welcome in both but the bookseller finally had to beg of him a favour: 'Next time you come down here why don't you come to the bookshop first and then go to the pub?'

When times were hard and the price of a pint hard to find, before the success of his plays, he painted the gents' at McDaid's for the price of a few pints. The manager recalled that he did a first-class job, evidence that the skills acquired when he was a guest of the British government had not been forgotten.

With his love of company and drink, the success of the plays, *The Hostage* and *The Quare Fellow*, was a mixed blessing. He recognized his own weakness when confiding to a friend over a pint or two: 'The trouble with me is I should be drinking stout all the time but I can afford spirits.'

He remained a true Dubliner, and a shrewd observer of the scene. Drink, he said, was no social disgrace for the poor: getting enough to eat was regarded as an achievement, getting drunk something of a victory.

He died, perhaps inevitably, too young. Brian O'Nolan, aka Flann O'Brien and Myles na Gopaleen, author of *At Swim-Two-Birds*, was a friend and fellow imbiber. After Behan's death he wrote: 'There has been no Irishman quite like him ... He exuded good nature. He excelled in language and was a total master of bad language. I have personally never heard the like of it. To use a Dublin saying, "he was as good as a play".'

Hold Your Hour and Have Another

Trails of Havoc

... An ancient, indestructible countenance, wrinkled and rugged enough to contain a shower of rain, but at present holding no more than the faintest traces of previous repasts of snuff, upturned itself from the inside of a shawl. 'Mrs. Jewel and darling, did I hear you say something?'

'I've to go and watch my grandchild's eldest, the Lotty one, get a couple of skips of fruit over to me pitch, the butt-end of Moore Street with her.'

'Still, and all, it was decent of her, and I looking for a bit of ground for me descendings. You might as well have a half in respect of her, not to mind Brending Behing being home, Me-Hall!'

'Yes, Mrs. Brennan, ma'am,' said Michael.

'Two pints of stout for the menkinds, and us ladies will have two half-ones and a bottle of Johnny-jump up.'[1] She turned to me. 'A surjing gave the tip. Lovely man, he was. Only for the ould drop. Too fond of it.

'Man sent up to be operated on for an ingrowing toenail. Me poor surjing read the card wrong and thought it was a head amputating was required. Amputated the head, God love him,

[1] A particularly potent cider that was on sale in Ireland up to about ten years ago.

very severe operating, the patiengt never come out of it and poor surjing was disgraced for life.'

'I knew one of them Swaines up in George's Packet, had his thumb amputated.'

'I remember them,' said Mrs. Brennan, 'they were married into the Leadbeaters.'

'That's right,' said Crippen, cheering himself up with a pull on his pint. 'Well, they were in a kind of religion that was very conscientious about the last day, and about getting up out of the grave, the way you were in this world. Well, Apollo Swaine …'

'Apollo?' I enquired.

'Yes, he got that name from hawking refreshments and shouting at the football matches, "Cigarettes, chocolate, toffee-app-oll-oh." Well, anyway, when he came out of the hospital he brought the thumb with him and gave a kind of little wake for it in Jimmy-The-Sports' Bar up on our corner.

'Had it on the counter beside him, bringing it up to bury it. "I'm going to put it where the rest of me will be when I die," says Apollo. "A fellow would look well on the last day, running round the nevin[2] like a half-thick and asking everyone, and they gathering up their ould traps themselves, "Ech, did you see e'er a sign of a thumb knocking round?" '

J P Donleavy

We have it on the authority of J P Donleavy himself that he was occasionally, in his youth, nearly as formidable a drinker as his famous anti-hero from *The Ginger Man*, Sebastian Dangerfield.

In his autobiographical *History of The Ginger Man* Donleavy describes his life as a student and budding writer in post-war Dublin. It was a world where excess was the norm: in drink, debts, womanizing, fighting, arguing. It's a belly laugh of a book, not recommended for reading in public as the snorts, chuckles and hoots of mirth it causes are likely to make people give you some very strange looks. The outrageous individuals in it – including the author – make the original characters of *The Ginger Man* seem like so many maiden aunts. Prominent among these individuals is Brendan Behan, described by Donleavy in frank but

[2] Glasnevin Cemetery.

affectionate terms: a lion-hearted drinker and 'pied piper, entertainer, sorcerer and conjurer'. They almost fought on their first meeting and had a memorable fist fight in the middle of Fleet Street during a prolonged pub-crawl of London.

Donleavy looks back on his first encounters with Irish stout, which he seems to have taken to at once:

> bartenders with sleeves rolled back handed the glasses over the heads as the rounds of drinks were bought and the sound of mechanical corkscrews twisted their way down with a thump and pop into the necks of the bottles of stout. And it was the name of this dark brew, stout, which confounded me when I first encountered it in James Joyce's writings. This beverage, which pumped blood through the hearts of the citizens and fuelled the city and ended up flowing through pub latrines, sewers and back to the Liffey from whose headwaters it had first come.

Donleavy has written many successful novels since *The Ginger Man*, but when it was first published some forty years ago Dangerfield set a new standard in bawdy, drunken, amoral, sex-hungry heroes. Generations of young men aspired to plumbing similar depths but few were fortunate enough to achieve it. *The Ginger Man* has been translated into twenty languages and continues to be a bestseller, having sold more than 10 million copies worldwide – figures to give any author a good reason for cracking open a celebratory bottle.

The Ginger Man lives on in a chain of American pubs in New York City, Dallas, Austin and Houston which all bear the name. These establishments, according to beer guru Michael Jackson, are some of the finest pubs in the States; they all sell beer from the barrel.

The mature J P Donleavy is fond of wine, especially champagne, and old champagne for preference, a taste which he recognizes is not shared by everyone – Roederer is a favourite marque. He's pretty catholic in his tastes. Of burgundy and claret, he says, 'I divide my loyalties between the two.'

But he has by no means disdained Ireland's 'black wine'. At his home in Ireland Donleavy has a bar complete with a Guinness pump from which he can dispense draught Guinness at will.

The Ginger Man

The bar was filled with old men. Spitting secrets in each other's ears. Smoke coming over the top of all the snugs. Faces turning as Dangerfield comes in. The sound of corks ripped pop. Ends of bottles bang on the bar. Seaweedy foam rising in the wet glasses. Rudeness must be dealt with. Swiftly. Put them down, I say, not up, down and don't spare the clubs.

Sebastian stepped to the bar, stood dignified and quiet. Bartender removing bottles. Comes along up to him. His eyes meeting the red ones and he nods his head to this tall customer.

'Yes?'

'A double Gold Label.'

Bartender turns a few steps and back with the bottle, tense and pouring.

'Water?'

'Soda.'

Bartender goes, gets the soda bottle. Squirt, squirt. A blast comes out of it. Whoops. The whiskey shot up the sides of the glass, splashing on the bar.

'Sorry, sir.'

'Yes.'

'It's a new bottle.'

'Quite.'

Bartender puts away the bottle and comes back for the money. Stands embarrassed in front of Dangerfield. Licking his lips, ready to speak, but waits, says nothing. Dangerfield looking at him. The old men sensing disaster, turning on their stools to watch.

'Two shillings.'

'I was in this public house this afternoon about four o'clock. Do you remember?'

'I do.'

'And you refused to serve me.'

'Yes.'

'On the grounds that I was drunk. Is that correct?'

'That's correct.'

'Do you think I am drunk now?'

'That's not for me to decide.'

'You decided that this afternoon. I repeat. Do you think I am drunk now?'

'I want no trouble.'

'Half my whiskey is on the bar.'

'No trouble now.'

'Would you mind bringing me the bottle to replace the amount splashed in my face.'

Bartender in his white shirt and sleeves rolled up brings back the bottle. Sebastian taking out the cork and filling his glass to the brim.

'You can't do that. We don't have much of that.'

'I repeat. Do you think I'm drunk now.'

'Now peacefully, no trouble, no trouble, we don't want any trouble here. No, I don't think you're drunk. Not drunk. Little excited. No.'

'I'm a sensitive person. I hate abuse. Let them all hear.'

'Quietly now, peace.'

'Shut up while I'm talking.'

All the figures spinning about on their stools and flat feet.

'No trouble now, no trouble.'

'Shut up. Am I drunk? Am I drunk?'

'No.'

'Why you Celtic lout. I am. I'm drunk. Hear me, I'm drunk and I'm going to level this kip, level it to the ground and anyone who doesn't want his neck broken get out.'

The whiskey bottle whistled past the bartender's head splattering in a mass of glass and gin. Dangerfield drank off the whiskey in a gulp and a man came up behind him with a stoutbottle which he broke on Dangerfield's head, stout dripping over his ears and down his face, reflectively licking it from around his mouth.

James Joyce

In a sense, James Joyce never left Ireland, despite living in exile from his homeland for most of his life. It can be said that he never wrote about anything else, his memory thronged with the people, places and pubs – especially the pubs – of his native city, Dublin. Bloom thinks how difficult it would be to cross Dublin without passing a pub, and many of them are featured by name in *Ulysses* – Mullet's in Amiens

Street, Dunphy's Corner in Bhisborough Road, Davy Byrne's in Duke Street and myriad others. For him and for Dubliners, drinking was a way of life, as it is still. Then and now the Guinness brewery dominated the city's commercial life, as glasses of 'the black stuff' dominate the bars.

Joyce remembered them: the deliveries of 'the dull-thudding Guinness barrels'. In *Ulysses* the Guinness operation is described:

> the foaming ebon ale which the noble twin brothers Bungiveagh and Bungardilaun brew ever in their divine elevats ... For they garner the succulent berries of the hop and mass and sift and bruise and brew them and they mix therewith sour juices and bring the must to the sacred fires and cease not night and day from toil, those cunning brothers, lords of the vat.

One Joycean scholar has described *Ulysses* as an 'archaeological/historical/anthropological/psychological novel', but it could just as well be described as a book about a tour through the bars of Dublin. Drink is a common preoccupation of many of the characters and the story has something of the flavour – sometimes hazy, sometimes starkly vivid – of a night on the town.

The characters are Dubliners. Oliver St John Gogarty, Buck Milligan in *Ulysses*, was supposed to have introduced Joyce to the pleasures of Guinness, but it is probable he would have discovered them for himself.

In any event, having discovered them, he explored them to the full in the company of Gogarty and other friends. It was with Gogarty that he found the title for his first collection of poems. They had taken them, with a supply of Guinness, to read to a merry widow. After the enjoyment of the poems and the drink, the good lady had to relieve herself in a chamber-pot behind a screen in the hearing of the two men. It was thus that the collection was given the title *Chamber Music*.

Joyce was a popular man in Dublin bars, not least because of his fine tenor voice. He once competed against the great John McCormack and often contemplated a career as a singer. His wife, the delightfully named Nora Barnacle, always said he would have done much better if he had taken that direction rather than trying to make a living by writing. Some anti-Joyceans say she has never been given her due as a literary critic.

When Joyce left Ireland, tired of its provincialism – he described it as his wife's 'native dunghill' – he does not appear to have missed any aspects of it very much, not even Guinness. In his wanderings in Europe, in Trieste, Rome, Zurich and Paris, he continued to drink habitually, loving the companionable nightlife of the cafés. His favourite drink was a Swiss white wine, Fendant de Sion, but he also enjoyed Neufchâtel, Riesling and white Chianti. Champagne enlivened many of his evenings in Paris. These drinks do not appear to have made the same deep impression on his memory as those of his youth in Dublin, although he never saw Ireland again after 1912.

Ulysses

All off for a buster, armstrong, hollering down the street. Bonafides. Where you slep las night? Timothy of the battered naggin. Like ole Billyo. Any brollies or gumboots in the fambly? Where the Henry Nevil's sawbones and ole clo? Sorra one of me knows. Hurrah there, Dix! Forward the ribbon counter. Where's Punch? All serene. Jay, look at the drunken minister coming out of the maternity hospal? *Benedicat vos omnipotens Deus, Pater et Filius*. A make, mister. The Denzille lane boys. Hell, blast ye! Scoot. Righto, Isaacs, shove em out of the bleeding limelight. Yous join uz, dead Sir? No hentrusion in life. Lou heap good man. Allee samee this bunch. *En avant, mes enfants!* Fire away number one on the gun. Burke's! Then they advanced five parasangs. Slattery's mounted foot where's that bleeding awfur? Parson Steve, apostates' creed! No, no, Mulligan! Abaft there! Shove ahead. Keep a watch on the clock. Chucking out time. Mullee! What's on you? *Ma mere m'a mariée*. British Beatitudes! *Retamplan Digidi Boum Boum*. Ayes have it. To be printed and bound at the Druiddrum press by two designing females. Calf covers of pissedon green. Last word in art shades. Most beautiful book come out of Ireland my time. *Silentium!* Get a spurt on. Tention. Proceed to nearest canteen and there annex liquor stores. March! Tramp, tramp, tramp, the boys are (attitudes) parching. Beer, beef, business, bibles, bulldogs, battleships, b—y and bishops. Whether on the scaffold high. Beerbeef trample the bibles. When for Ireelandear. Trample the trampellers. Thunderation! Keep the durned millingtary step. We fall. Bishops boosebox. Halt! Heave to. Rugger. Scrum in. No touch kicking. Wow, my tootsies! You hurt? Most amazing sorry!

Query. Who's astanding this here do? Proud possessor of damnall. Declare misery. Bet to the ropes. Me nantee saltee. Not a red at me this week gone. Yours? Mead of our fathers for the *Uebermensch*. Dittoh. Five number ones. You sir? Ginger cordial. Chase me, the cabby's caudle. Stimulate the caloric. Winding of the ticker. Stopped short never to go again when the old. Absinthe for me, savvy? *Caramba!* Have an eggnog or a prairie oyster. Enemy? Avuncular's got my timepiece. Ten to. Obligated awful. Don't mention it. Got a pectoral trauma, eh, Dix? Pos fact. Got bet be a boomblebee whenever he was setting sleeping in hes bit garten. Digs up near the mater. Buckled he is. Know his dona? Yup, sartin, I do. Full of a dure. See her in her dishybilly. Peels off a credit. Lovey lovekin. None of your lean kine, not much. Pull down the blind, love. Two Ardilauns. Same here. Look slippery. If you fall don't wait to get up. Five, seven, nine. Fine! Got a prime pair of mincepies, no kid. And her take me to rests and her anker of rum. Must be seen to be believed. Your starving eyes and allbeplastered neck you stole my heart. O gluepot. Sir? Spud again the rheumatiz? All poppycock, you'l scuse me saying. For the hoi polloi. I vear thee beest a gert wool. Well, doc? Back fro Lapland? Your corporosity sagaciating OK? How's the squaws and papooses? Womanbody after going on the straw? Stand and deliver. Password. There's hair. Ours the white death and the ruddy birth. Hi! Spit in your eye, boss. Mummer's wire. Cribbed out of Meredith. Jesified orchidised polycimical jesuit! Aunty mine's writing Pa Kinch. Baddybad Stephen lead astray goodygood Malachi.

Hurroo! Collar the leather, youngun. Roun wi the nappy. Here, Jock braw Hielentman's your barleybree. Lang may your lum reek and your kailpot boil! My tipple. *Merci*. Here's to us. How's that? Leg before wicket. Don't stain my brandnew sitinems. Give's a shake of pepper, you there. Catch aholt. Caraway seed to carry away. Twig? Shrieks of silence. Every cove to his gentry mort. Venus Pandemos. *Les petites femmes*. Bold bad girl from the town of Mullingar. Tell her I was axing at her. Hauding Sara by the wame. On the road to Malahide. Me? If she who seduced me had left but the name. What do you want for ninepence. Machree, Macruiskeen. Smutty Moll for a mattress jig. And a pull altogether. *Ex!*

... You move a motion? Steve boy, you're going it some. More bluggy drunkables? Will immensely splendiferous stander permit one stooder of most extreme poverty and one largesize grandacious thirst to terminate one expensive inaugurated libation? Give's a breather. Landlord, landlord, have you good wine, staboo? Hoots, mon, wee drap to pree. Cut and come again. Right Boniface! Absinthe the lot. *Nos omnes biberimus viridum toxicum diabolus capiat posterioria nostria*. Closingtime, gents. Eh? Rome boose for the Bloom toff. I hear you say onions? Bloo? Cadges ads? Photo's papli, by all that's gorgeous. Play low, pardner. Slide. *Bonsoir la campagnie*. And snares of the poxfiend. Where's the buck and Namby Amby? Skunked? Leg bail. Aweel, ye maun e'en gang her gates. Checkmate. King to tower. Kind Kristyann will yu help, yung man hoose frend tuk bungalo kee to find plais whear to lay crown off his hed 2 night. Crickey, I'm about sprung. Tarnally dog gone my shins if this beent the bestest puttiest longbreak yet. Item, curate, couple of cookies for this child. Cot's plood and prandypalls none! Not a pite of sheeses? Thrust syphilis down to hell and with him those other licensed spirits. Time. Who wander through the world. Health all. *A la votre*.

Golly, whatten tunket's you guy in the mackintosh? Dusty Rhodes. Peep at his wearables. By mighty! Jubilee mutton. Bovril, by James. Wants it real bad. D'ye ken bare socks? Seedy cuss in the Richmond? Rawthere! Thought he had a deposit of lead in his penis. Trumpery insanity. Battle the Bread we calls him. That, sir, was once a prosperous cit. Man all tattered and torn that married a maiden all forlorn. Slung her hook, she did. Here see lost love. Walking Mackintosh of lonely canyon. Tuck and turn in. Schedule time. Nix for the hornies. Pardon? See him today at a runefal? Chum of yourn passed in his checks? Ludamassy! Pore piccanninies! Thou'll no be telling me thot, Pold veg! Did ums blubble big-splash crytears cos frien Padney was took off in black bag? Of all de darkies Massa Pat was verra best. I never see the like since I was born. *Tiens, tiens*, but it is well sad, that, my faith, yes. O get, rev on a gradient one in nine. Live axle drives are souped. Lay you two to one Jenatzy licks him ruddy well hollow. Jappies? High angle fire, inyah! Sunk by war specials. Be worse for him, say he, nor any Rooshian. Time all. There's eleven of them. Get ye gone. Forward, woozy wobblers! Night. Night. May Allah, the Excellent One, your soul this night ever tremendously conserve.

Flann O'Brien

The author of *At Swim-Two-Birds* was a triumvirate: Flann O'Brien, novelist; Myles na Gopaleen, newspaper columnist; and Brian O'Nolan, civil servant. It may be that these names expressed different aspects of a single personality, but they had one thing in common: as they say in Ireland, they were fond of a drop.

It was a taste easily indulged in that most hospitable of cities, Dublin. As a student at Trinity in the 1920s O'Brien and his friends foregathered at Grogan's, close to the college entrance, where a pint of plain porter was 4½*d* and a pint of stout 7*d*. O'Nolan was regarded as a brilliant man at Trinity but his views of the university were neither sentimental nor favourable. Later in life, as Myles na Goppaleen, he recalled that it was all 'a sham':

> The only result my father got for his money was the certainty that his son had laid faultlessly the foundation of a system of heavy drinking and could always be relied upon to make a break of at least 25 even with a bad cue.

He had a similarly jaundiced view of *At Swim-Two-Birds* which he dismissed as juvenilia, even though it was admired by James Joyce and Graham Greene and is currently enjoyed by every right-thinking citizen in Ireland and Britain. 'It is a bellylaugh or a high-class literary pretentious slush depending on how you look at it,' he wrote.

Admirers have no such doubts and find its style, as shown in this delicious fragment, irresistible:

> I was sitting on a stool in an intoxicated condition in Grogan's licensed premises. Adjacent stools bore the forms of Brinsley and Sheridan, my two true friends. The three of us were occupied in putting glasses of stout into the interior of our bodies and expressing by fine disputation the resulting sense of physical and mental well being.

The characters in the novel are often drawn from life. O'Brien's biographer, the poet Anthony Cronin, says the character of Byrne was based on the Dublin painter Cecil French-Salkeld. He was a notable figure who spent much of his time in bed drinking whiskey – a habit O'Brien was to develop in later life – and only rising on significant occasions, such as the annual cleaning of murals he had painted in Dave Byrne's pub off Grafton Street.

O'Brien was a civil servant for much of his life, which was why he published pseudonymously. By all accounts, he was highly competent and rose steadily through the ranks. It was only towards the end of his career that drinking, and possibly boredom, affected his performance.

Dublin was a paradise for drinkers then, as it is today. O'Brien – or Myles, as he was generally known – knew many of the pubs and was almost a part of the furniture in a number of them. Grogan's, Davy Byrne's, the Palace Bar, the Pearl, McDaid's, the Scotch House (well known for fine whiskey, not whisky despite its name, the drink favoured by the mature O'Nolan) were all regular ports of call. It was in these places that he exchanged drinks, witticisms and insults with assorted Dublin literati such as Patrick Kavanagh and Brendan Behan. Everybody drank heavily, and O'Brien's drinking must have been unremarkable in circles of this kind. He was normally quiet, even a little shy when sober, so that Brendan Behan (who was neither of these things) said, 'You had to look twice to see if he was there at all.'

For most of his life O'Brien was little known outside Ireland and then mainly to readers of the *Irish Times* for whom he wrote his satirical column as Myles na Gopaleen. Wider appreciation came later but he did not become famous until after his death on 1 April 1966: April Fool's Day, a date he might have noted with mordant enjoyment.

He is remembered by Dubliners as a cherished Dublin character with a sharp wit. While engaged in one of the many controversies that were a part of his life as Myles na Gopaleen he was described as having become a 'super-bishop'. O'Brien replied, 'Really, I have no ecclesiastical ambitions … I am merely a spoiled Proust.'

At Swim-Two-Birds

Biographical reminiscence, part the first: It was only a few months before composing the foregoing that I had my first experience of intoxicating beverages and their strange intestinal chemistry. I was walking through the Stephen's Green on a summer evening and conducting a conversation with a man called Kelly, then a student, hitherto a member of the farming class and now a private in the armed forces of the King. He was addicted to unclean expressions in ordinary conversation and spat continually, always fouling the flowerbeds on his way through the Green with a mucous deposit dislodged with a low grunting from the interior of his windpipe. In some respects he was a coarse man but he was lacking in malice or ill-humour. He purported to be a medical student but he had failed at least once to satisfy a body of examiners charged with regulating admission to the faculty. He suggested that we should drink a number of *jars* or pints of plain porter in Grogan's public house. I derived considerable pleasure from the casual quality of his suggestion and observed that it would probably do us no harm, thus expressing my wholehearted concurrence by a figure of speech.

Name of figures of speech: Litotes (or Meiosis)

He turned to me with a facetious wry expression and showed me a penny and a sixpence in his rough hand.

I'm thirsty, he said. I have sevenpence. Therefore I buy a pint.

I immediately recognized this as an intimation that I should pay for my own porter.

The conclusion of your syllogism, I said lightly, is fallacious, being based on licensed premises.

Licensed premises is right, he replied, spitting heavily. I saw that my witticism was unperceived and quietly replaced it in the treasury of my mind.

We sat in Grogan's with our faded overcoats finely disarrayed on easy chairs in the mullioned snug. I gave a shilling and two pennies to a civil man who brought us in return two glasses of black porter, imperial pint measure. I adjusted the glasses to the front of each of us and reflected on the solemnity of the occasion. It was my first taste of porter. Innumerable persons with whom I had conversed had represented to me that spirituous liquors and intoxicants generally had an adverse effect on the senses and the body and that those who became addicted to stimulants in youth were unhappy throughout their lives and met with death at the end by a drunkard's fall, expiring ingloriously at the stair-bottom in a welter of blood and puke. Indian tonic-waters had been proposed to me by an aged lay-brother as an incomparable specific for thirst. The importance of the subject had been impressed upon me in a school-book which I read at the age of twelve.

... On the other hand, young men of my acquaintance who were in the habit of voluntarily placing themselves under the influence of alcohol had often surprised me with a recital of their strange adventures. The mind may be impaired by alcohol, I mused, but withal it may be pleasantly impaired. Personal experience appeared to me to be the only satisfactory means to the resolution of my doubts. Knowing it was my first one, I quietly fingered the butt of my glass before I raised it.

T L Peacock

Thomas Love Peacock is not a name that is much spoken of these days, except perhaps by academics and a few fusty eccentrics with a liking for nineteenth-century literature.

His best-known lines are probably the following, but even these are often attributed to other writers:

Not drunk is he, who from the floor
Can rise alone, and still drink more;
But drunk is he, who prostrate lies,
Without the power to drink or rise.

All of which is a pity because Peacock is a genuinely funny writer about the world in which he lived and the part drink played in it.

Beginning as a poet, as so many literary men do he shook off the influences of a close friendship with Shelley, finding his own voice in a number of novels with characters such as Prince Seighenyn ap Seithyn Saidi in *The Misfortunes of Elphin*. Described by Peacock as 'one of the three immortal drunkards of the isle of Britain', Seithyn believes that wine is a powerful aid to comprehending truth: 'Wine from gold has a sort of double light, that illuminates a dark path miraculously,' he declares.

Another character is Dr Folliott in *Crotchet Castle*, 'a gentleman endowed with a tolerable stock of learning, an interminable swallow and an indefatigable pair of lungs', who is said to be a self-portrait of Peacock himself. The doctor certainly shares many of the author's enthusiasms, especially for food and drink. The character was described by J B Priestley as an Epicurean: 'If there is ever an Epicurean Church, he should be one of its saints'; a remark that could well be applied to T L Peacock.

Convincing evidence of his attitude towards drink can be found in the work of the novelist George Meredith, who married Peacock's daughter, Mary. Some scholars claim that the character of Dr Middleton in *The Egoist* bears such a strong family resemblance to Peacock/Dr Folliott that it must be a portrait of him. The good Dr Middleton is a man of many fine qualities, learning and charity, but these are as nothing beside his deep and abiding passion for vintage port.

Peacock appears to have been a wise, humorous individual who much enjoyed poking fun at popular but gloomy figures of the period such as Coleridge and Byron. He is eminently sane and highly quotable, as in this from Mr Hilary, a character in *Nightmare Abbey*:

> To rail against humanity for not being abstract perfection, and against human love for not realising all the splendid visions of the poets of chivalry, is to rail at the summer for not being all sunshine, and at the rose for not being always in bloom.

Headlong Hall

Mr CRANIUM. Pardon me: it is here. – (*As he said these words, he produced a skull from his pocket, and placed it on the table, to the great surprise of the company.*) – This was the skull of Sir Christopher Wren. You observe this protuberance – (*The skull was handed round the table.*)

Mr ESCOT. I contend that the original unsophisticated man was by no means constructive. He lived in the open air, under a tree.

The REVEREND DOCTOR GASTER. The tree of life. Unquestionably. Till he had tasted the forbidden fruit.

Mr JENKINSON. At which period, probably, the organ of constructiveness was added to his anatomy, as a punishment for his transgression.

Mr ESCOT. There could not have been a more severe one, since the propensity which has led him to building cities has proved the greatest curse of his existence.

Squire HEADLONG – (*taking the skull*) *Memento mori*. Come, a bumper of Burgundy.

Mr NIGHTSHADE. A very classical application, Squire Headlong. The Romans were in the practice of adhibiting skulls at their banquets, and sometimes little skeletons of silver, as a silent admonition to the guest to enjoy life while it lasted.

The REVEREND DOCTOR GASTER. Sound doctrine, Mr Nightshade.

Mr ESCOT. I question its soundness. The use of vinous spirit has a tremendous influence in the deterioration of the human race.

Mr FOSTER. I fear, indeed, it operates as a considerable check to the progress of the species towards moral and intellectual perfection. Yet many great men have been of opinion that it exalts the imagination, fires the genius, accelerates the flow of ideas, and imparts to dispositions naturally cold and deliberative that enthusiastic sublimation which is the source of greatness and energy ...

Mr JENKINSON. I conceive the use of wine to be always pernicious in excess, but often useful in moderation: it certainly kills some, but it saves the lives of others: I find that an occasional glass, taken with judgment and caution, has a very salutary effect in maintaining that equilibrium of the system, which it is always my aim to preserve.

Edgar Allan Poe

If the terrifying, macabre visions that haunt the tales of Edgar Allan Poe were the result of excessive drinking they would make a potent argument for swearing off alcohol. It is hard to imagine a more gruesome depiction of the consequence of drinking than in his short story, 'The Black Cat', when the narrator returns home 'much intoxicated'. He seizes the cat which gives him a minor wound:

> The fury of a demon instantly possessed me ... I knew myself no longer ... and a more than fiendish malevolence, gin-nurtured, thrilled every fibre of my frame. I took from my waistcoat pocket a pen-knife, opened it, grasped the poor beast by the throat, and deliberately cut one of its eyes from the socket.

NEVERMORE...
E·A·Poe

There is no evidence, however, that drink fuelled his fevered imagination, or created the desperately black world of his fiction. It simply seems to have been part of Poe's make-up, like the colour of his eyes or his size in shoes. At college he gained a reputation for hard drinking, a fellow-student noting the way he drank the peach-and-honey-flavoured Southern punch: 'It was not the taste of the beverage that influenced him; without a sip or a smack of the mouth he would seize a full glass, and send it home at a single gulp.'

Contemporaries from his brief spell at West Point remembered sessions of brandy-drinking on illicit expeditions from the barracks.

Poe's partiality for drink began to lead him into trouble. He was sacked from a newspaper for being drunk and given sound advice by his employer: 'no man is safe who drinks before breakfast'.

There were lengthy periods when he did not drink at all. In answer to further charges of drunkenness, Poe claimed he had not taken any alcohol for four years: 'with the exception of a single deviation ... when I was induced to resort to the occasional use of cider, with the hope of relieving a nervous attack'.

But he did eventually resort to alcohol again, with damaging effects. The trouble was that he was highly susceptible to alcohol and it had a huge effect on his nervous, volatile temperament. With hindsight we can say he might have been wiser to abstain from alcohol, to turn away from it with the words of the raven in what is probably his most famous poem, 'Nevermore'.

Bon-Bon

'Were you ever at Rome?' asked the *restaurateur*, as he finished his second bottle of Mousseux, and drew from the closet a larger supply of Chambertin.

'But once, Monsieur Bon-Bon, but once. There was a time,' said the Devil, as if reciting some passage from a book – 'there was a time when occurred an anarchy of five years, during which the republic, bereft of all its officers had no magistracy besides the tribunes of the people, and these were not legally vested with any degree of executive power – at that time, Monsieur Bon-Bon – at that time *only* I was in Rome, and I have no earthly acquaintance, consequently, with any of its philosophy.'

'What do you think of – what do you think of – hiccup! –

Epicurus!'

'What do I think of *whom*?' said the Devil, in astonishment; 'you surely do not mean to find any fault with Epicurus! What do I think of Epicurus! Do you mean me, sir? – I am Epicurus! I am the same philosopher who wrote each of the three hundred treatises commemorated by Diogenes Laertes.'

'That's a lie!' said the metaphysician, for the wine had gotten a little into his head.

'Very well! – very well, sir! very well indeed, sir!' said his Majesty, apparently much flattered.

'That's a lie!' repeated the *restaurateur*, dogmatically; 'that's a – hicup! – a lie!'

'Well, well, have it your own way!' said the Devil, pacifically, and Bon-Bon, having beaten his Majesty at an argument, thought it his duty to conclude a second bottle of Chambertin.

'As I was saying,' resumed the visitor, 'as I was observing a little while ago, there are some very *outré* notions in that book of yours, Monsieur Bon-Bon. What for instance, do you mean by all that humbug about the soul? Pray, Sir, what *is* the soul?'

'The – hiccup! – soul,' replied the metaphysician, referring to his MS., 'is undoubtedly—'

'No, sir!'

'Indubitably—'

'No, sir!'

'Indisputably—'

'No, sir!'

'Evidently—'

'No, sir!'

'Incontrovertibly—'

'No, sir!'

'Hiccup!'

'No, sir!'

'And beyond the question, a—'

'No, sir, the soul is no such thing!' (Here the philosopher, looking daggers, took occasion to make an end, upon the spot, of his third bottle of Chambertin.)

'Then – hiccup! – pray, sir – what – what is it?'

'That is neither here nor there, Monsieur Bon-Bon,' replied his Majesty musingly. 'I have tasted – that is to say, I have known some very bad souls, and some too – pretty good ones.' Here he smacked his lips, and having unconsciously let fall his hand upon the volume in his pocket, was seized with a violent fit of sneezing.

He continued:

'There was the soul of Cratinus – passable; Aristophanes – racy; Plato – exquisite – not *your* Plato, but Plato the comic poet; your Plato would have turned the stomach of Cerberus – faugh! Then let me see! There were Naevius, and Andronicus, and Plautus, and Terentius. Then there was Lucilius, and Catullus, and Naso, and Quintus Flaccus – dear Quinty! as I called him when he sang a *seculare* for my amusement while I toasted him, in pure good humour, on a fork. But they want *flavour*, these Romans. One fat Greek is worth a dozen of them, and besides will *keep*, which cannot be said of a Quirite. Let us taste your Sauterne.'

J B Priestley

Distinguished writers are, almost by definition, a little odd. The more gifted they are, it seems, the more likely they are to be, let us say, a touch unworldly, eccentric or just plain daft. Despite being just about as distinguished as it is possible to be, J B Priestley is unusual in the annals of literature in that he is eminently sane.

His sanity is evident in his approach to drink, which he thoroughly enjoyed. He did not take a sanctimonious, mealymouthed or even romantic attitude towards it – it was simply there, to be used, just as other good things in life such as food and sex.

As a quintessential Yorkshireman – almost a professional Yorkshireman, cynics sometimes suggested – he was hardnosed and hardheaded, qualities that were evident in the way he coped with drink. Although his father was an enthusiastic member of the Baptist chapel, he was familiar with the pubs of his birthplace, Bradford, and their place in the lives of working men. In time, he came to celebrate the pleasures of beer and companionship in print, notably in *The Good Companions* (a huge bestseller which earned him the equivalent of around £600,000).

Strong drink was as much a part of London literary life in the 1920s as it is today, perhaps more so. Aspiring writers and journalists gravitated to pubs in Fleet Street and Soho to pay court to established members of the profession, hoping to pick their brains and to pick up the odd commission – and it worked.

Apart from pubs, there were eating places in Soho in the 1920s where 10 shillings would buy a meal with wine, brandy and cigars. These establishments were much patronized by Priestley, who was a considerable trencherman.

His taste in drink tended towards spirits, although he took wine with his meals. A concoction called a Dog's Nose, not often seen in these more enlightened days, was a favourite. It is a very potent mixture of gin and beer, and it is not surprising that after a supply of these Priestley was more than happy to be persuaded to the piano to thump out items from his wide repertoire of popular tunes.

Lucky enough to have a robust constitution, he was able to recover quite readily from the effects of drinks such as firewater whiskey with locals in the American Midwest when lecturing there and endless glasses of vodka when visiting Tiflis, Georgia. He was not, it must be said, completely unaffected by these celebrations, admitting that on the latter occasion he recited Hamlet's dying speech 'without provocation' and on another joining PEN after dining with Galsworthy and imbibing 'so much drink – no rough stuff with whisky bottles but a stately procession from dry sherry to port and brandy – that I would have scrawled a signature to anything'.

Drinking Time

When I first arrived in London in the early 1920s I was introduced to a lot of hard drinking, in and around Fleet Street. The talk was probably the best I have ever heard, but it was nourished by round after round of 'doubles'. The hardest drinkers kept to whisky, and I remember a very influential man of letters, staying with me, drinking a whole bottle *before lunch*. Oddly enough, these men neither neglected their work (though they ought to have been writing books instead of articles and reviews) nor died young; and I cannot remember one of them ever being quarrelsome and bellicose. And unlike the next generation of literary critics, they were never pompous, priggish and arrogant. They floated gently from office to pub to desk to book to pub again.

There was even harder and more dangerous drinking, I found, in America under Prohibition. This was the only time I have drunk whisky and gin – very strong, and dubious – in the middle of the morning. I would call, let us say, about ten-thirty on a publisher or editor, and he would immediately announce that he had 'something very special, just off the boat' and to refuse a drink or two would have been insulting. A day begun like that could end at two in the morning, in a speakeasy owned by gangsters. As bad mistakes that went on and on, Prohibition and Vietnam get the prizes.

Recently I have read some rather ominous statements by medical men equating hard drinking – incidentally, not one of my weaknesses – with alcoholism. Both may want to blur reality, but one is an expensive and stupid habit, the other a disease. Hard drinkers enjoy booze; alcoholics hate it but must have it. My wife, an authority on the distant past, tells me that men just emerging from the mists of lost time were already busy fermenting intoxicating drink. No doubt we abuse our liberty to take in alcohol. But then we abuse our liberty to set cars in motion. In fact, we abuse our liberty, being imperfect creatures. But not so many people would want to blur reality with drink, boozing not out of sociability but out of desperation, if the reality we have created were less forbidding.

My advice now, coming out of long experience, is addressed to young men. Never never drink hard when you are filled with self-pity and miserable. Give yourself a job, even if it is only painting some bookshelves. Unless there is some hereditary taint, you will never become an alcoholic if you do no drinking until you have done your day's work. If you have to prime yourself to get the work done, sooner or later you will be in bad trouble. Two fine actors I have known were in the sharpest contrast here. One of them, still in magnificent form, never takes a drink until the final curtain is down, and then, his work well done, he will pour out gin as if it were water. The other needed a whole bottle of gin just to get through a performance, and after many a disaster he died. Strong drink is not a medicine; it is a bonus, a spirit to lift our spirit a little but never to quench it.

François Rabelais

Rabelais is one of a rare company of writers – Chaucer and Joyce are others – whose names have spawned adjectives. Rabelaisian, as everybody knows – including those who have never read a word by him – means a vigorous, outspoken celebration of the physical delights of life; particularly food and drink.

Scholars claim that the works of Rabelais are moralistic in intention, that the fizzing descriptions of wine and food are symbols; drink, for example, is said to represent a thirst for knowledge. But for most people Rabelais remains a poet of the pleasures of indulgence.

The first words uttered by the giant Gargantua are 'Drink! Drink! Drink!' Pantagruel's army (his name means all-thirst) has the slogan 'hand on pot and glass in fist' and his warriors are much more interested in eating and drinking than soldiering. The more they eat and drink the more the talk flows in puns and vulgar jokes. The tone is, well, Rabelaisian – one character muses, 'There is no shade like that of curtains, no smoke like steaming breasts, and no clattering like that of ballocks.' A young man calls his girlfriend 'My mattress', and she calls him her counterpane; another addresses his girl as 'my shovel' and she responds by calling him 'my poker'.

Rabelais was born in the town of Chinon, towards the end of the fifteenth century. Chinon was and is famous for its wine, and tradition has it that Rabelais had a vineyard where he made what he described as 'taffeta' wines, soft and velvety. It's a good description of Chinon wines of today, which are also said to smell of violets, but intensive research by this writer has revealed only a consistent bouquet of wine.

A statue of Rabelais stands in the town, below the ruined medieval chateau overlooking the placid, tree-fringer River Vienne. It depicts a substantial man with a dignified bearing, as befits a monk who was a doctor of medicine. It is a pleasing tradition to pay homage to the great man by toasting him with a draught of cool Chinon wine, perhaps similar to that he promised to a friend: 'good wine kept here against your coming'.

Gargantua and Pantagruel

What difference is there between a bottle and a flaggon? A great difference, for the bottle is stopped and shut up with a stopper, but the flaggon with a vice, bravely and well plaid upon the words. Our fathers drank lustily, and emptied their cans; well cack'd, well sung; come, let us drink: will you send nothing to the river, here is one going to wash the tripes: I drink no more then a spunge, I drink like a Templar Knight: and I *tanquam sponsus* and I, *sicut terra sine aqua*; give me a synonymon for a gammon of bacon? it is the compulsory of drinkers: it is a pully; by a pully-rope wine is let down into a cellar, and by a gammon into the stomack; hei! now boyes hither, some drink, some drink, there is no trouble in it, *respice personam, pone pro duos, bus non est in usu*. If I could get up as well as I can swallow down, I had been long ere now very high in the aire.

Thus became Tom Tosse-pot rich, thus went in the Taylors stitch; thus did Bacchus conquer th'Inde, thus Philosophy Melinde: a little raine allayes a great deal of winde: long tipling breaks the thunder. But if there came such liquor from my ballock, would you not willingly thereafter suck the udder when it issued; here, page, fill; I prethee, forget me not when it comes to my turne, and I will enter the election I have made of thee into the very register of my heart; sup, Guillot, and spare not, there is yet somewhat in the pot. I appeale from thirst, and disclaim its jurisdiction. Page, sue out my appeale in forme, this remnant in the bottome of the glasse must follow its Leader. I was wont heretofore to drink out all, but now I leave nothing. Let us not make too much haste, it is requisite we carry all along with us; heyday, here are tripes fit for our sport, and in earnest excellent Godebillios of the dun Oxe (you know) with the black streak. O for God's sake let us lash them soundly, yet thriftily. Drink, or I will. No, no, drink I beseech you; sparrows will not eate unless you bob them on the taile, nor can I drink if I be not fairly spoken to. The concavities of my body are like another Hell for their capacity. Lagonaedatera, there is not a corner, nor cunniborow in all my body where this wine doth not ferret out my thirst. Ho, this will bang it soundly, but this shall banish it utterly. Let us winde our hornes by the sound of flaggons and bottles, and cry aloud, that whoever hath lost his thirst, come not hither to seek it. Long cylsters of drinking are to be voided without doors: the great God made the Planets, and we make the platters neat. I have the word of the Gospel in my mouth, Sitio. The stone called Asbests, is not more unquenchable, then the thirst of my paternitie. Appetitle comes with eating saies Angeston, but thirst goes away with drinking. I have a remedy against thirst, quite contrary to that which is good against the biting of a mad dog. Keep running after a Dog, and he will never bite you. There I catch you, I awake you.

Argus had a hundred eyes for his sight, a butler should have (like Briareus) a hundred hands wherewith to fill us wine indefatigably. Hey now, lads, let us moisten our selves, it will be time to dry hereafter. Whie wine here, wine boyes, poure out all in the name of Lucifer, fill here you, fill and fill (pescods on you) till it be full. My tongue peels. Lanstrinque, to thee, Countreyman, I drink to thee good fellow, camarade to thee, lustie, lively.

R B Sheridan

There are so many anecdotes about Richard Brinsley Sheridan's drinking that he could almost merit an anthology of his own.

The painter Benjamin Haydon recounted a time when Sheridan and others were dining at Somerset House and were thoroughly enjoying the evening when a servant rushed in, shouting, 'Sir, the house is on fire!'

'Bring another bottle of claret,' said Sheridan amiably. 'It is not my house.'

When his own Drury Lane Theatre was in flames and he was faced with financial disaster he watched the conflagration calmly, glass in hand. A bystander commented on his fortitude and Sheridan shrugged and smiled, saying, 'A man may surely take a glass of wine by his own fireside.'

His reputation even invaded the pages of fiction, a character in Thackeray's *Pendennis* referring to seeing Sheridan 'drink five bottles at Brookes's, besides a bottle of Maraschino'.

There was, indeed, something almost fictional about his life. He jumps off the pages of biography, fizzing with energy and purpose. By the time he was 30 he had written a string of successful plays, including *The Rivals* and *The School for Scandal*. He became a theatre owner, made a fortune and promptly lost it.

Political success was his real goal. He became an MP, and was soon known as Parliament's most famous orator. He was intimate with the mighty, including the Prince of Wales, who was said to drink as much as Sheridan.

In an age when debt was common he was a champion debtor, running up bills of thousands of pounds, never opening letters, his affairs in total confusion. He was constantly pursued by creditors but had a cool nerve. When caught in The Mall by one of them he stopped and admired the creditor's horse.

'Oh,' said Sheridan, 'that's a beautiful mare you are on.'

'D'ye think so?'

'Yes, indeed, how does she trot?'

The creditor, quite delighted, told him he should see, and immediately put her into full trotting pace. The instant he trotted off, Sheridan turned into Pall Mall again and was out of sight in a moment.

But he survived, delighting his many friends with his company, talking and drinking the nights away. The young Lord Byron met Sheridan when the playwright was an old man but remembered: 'Poor dear Sherry. I shall never forget the day when he and Rogers and Moore and I passed together; when he talked and we listened, without one yawn, from six till one in the morning.'

Of course, his talk was not as magical when in his cups but his wit remained. A watchman found him one night, much the worse for drink. 'Who are you, sir?' he asked. There was no answer. 'What's your name?' The answer was a hiccup. 'What's your name?' At last the answer came in a slow, deliberate voice: 'Wilberforce!' (Wilberforce was the eminent opponent of slavery and a teetotaller.)

His fortune rose and, inevitably, fell, and he died in poverty at the age of 65. Byron, who had a similar love of life, said he had written the best comedy, the best opera, the best farce and the best oration 'ever conceived or heard in this country'. He remembered, too, 'he was a clever fellow and that we have had some very pleasant days with him'.

The School for Scandal

CHARLES – CARELESS – *ETC. ETC. AT A TABLE WITH WINE ETC.*

CHARLES 'Fore heaven, 'tis true – there's the great Degeneracy of the age – many of our acquaintance have Taste, spirit, and Politeness – but plague on't they won't drink.

CARELESS It is so indeed Charles – they give into all the substantial Luxuries of the Table – and abstain from nothing but wine and wit—

CHARLES O certainly Society suffers by it intolerably – for now instead of the social spirit of Raillery that used to mantle over a glass of bright Burgundy their conversation is become just like the Spa water they drink which has all the Pertness and flatulence of Champaine without its Spirit or Flavour—

1ST GENT But what are they to do who love Play better than wine?

CARELESS True – there's Harry diets himself – for Gaming and is now under a Hazard – regimen—

CHARLES Then He'll have the worst of it – what you wouldn't train a horse for the course by keeping him from corn – for my Part egad I am now – never so successful as when I am a little – merry – let me throw on a Bottle of Champaine and I never lose – at least I never feel my losses which is exactly the same thing.

2ND GENT Aye – that I believe.

CHARLES And then what man can pretend to be a Believer in Love who is an abjuror of Wine & 'tis the Test by which the Lover knows his own Heart, fill a dozen Bumpers to a dozen Beauties – and she that floats at top is the Maid that has bewitch'd you—

CARELESS Now then Charles – be honest and give us your real favorite—

CHARLES Why I have withheld her only in compassion to you – if I toast her you must give a round of her Peers which is impossible! on earth!

CARELESS O then we'll find some canonized Vestals or heathen Goddess that will do I warrant—

CHARLES Here then – Bumpers – you Rogues – Bumpers! – Maria – Maria – (*drink*)

1ST GENT Maria who?

CHARLES O damn the Surname! 'tis too formal to be register'd in Love's Calendar – out now Sir Toby Bumper beware – we must have Beauty superlative.

CARELESS Nay never Study Sir Toby – we'll Stand to The Toast – tho' your mistress should want an Eye – and you know you have a song will excuse you—

SIR TOBY Egad so I have – and I'll give him the Song instead of the Lady—

Song and Chorus

Here's to the maiden of Bashful fifteen
  Here's to the Widow of Fifty
Here's to the flaunting, Extravagant Queen,

And here's to the House Wife that's thrifty.
Let the toast pass –
Drink to the lass –
I'll warrant She'll prove an Excuse for the Glass!

2d.

Here's to the Charmer whose Dimples we Prize!
Now to the Maid who has none Sir;
Here's to the Girl with a pair of blue Eyes,
And Here's to the Nymph with but one Sir!
Let the Toast pass etc.

3d.

Here's to the Maid with a Bosom of Snow,
Now to her that's as brown as a berry;
Here's to the Wife with face full of Woe,
And now for the Damsel that's Merry.
Let the Toast pass etc.

4th.

For let 'Em be Clumsy or let 'Em be Slim
Young or Ancient, I care not a Feather;
So fill a Pint Bumper Quite up to the Brim
And let us E'en toast 'Em together!
Let the Toast pass etc.

John Squire

It would be forgivable for the modern reader to guess that Sir John Squire might have had a bit part in *Henry IV*: a boozing chum of Falstaff, a soldier, a sound man, despite his partiality for drink and whoring.

In fact, he was a literary man, a poet and man of letters, who died as recently as 1958. In his day Sir John Squire was a power in the literary landscape; indeed, in the 1920s he and his cronies dominated magazines and journals like a literary Mafia which was known as the 'Squirearchy'.

His writings, his poems and essays, are long forgotten but he has the great distinction of having served as a model for characters by Evelyn Waugh and A G MacDonnell. His Jack Spire in *Decline and Fall* is a minor role, it is true, but he takes centre stage as Hodge, the captain of the nomadic cricket team in *England, Their England*, that classic of the coarse cricket, and it is to him the book is dedicated: to J C Squire, the English poet.

The character is closely modelled on Squire, who captained a wandering cricket team called The Invalids which was made up of authors, critics, sub-editors and various literary types – often augmented by spectators to take the place of players who had failed to turn up, and even, on one occasion, the taxi-driver who had delivered a player to the ground.

According to Alec Waugh, who played against the team several times, there is no exaggeration in the scenes depicted: 'It really was like that,' he said. He remembered Squire's bowling with astonishment: 'He took a four-step trot, and tossed high into the air a ball guileless of spin and swerve.' Squire was a generous, open-handed man; 'his problem was conviviality,' said Waugh. He was always ready to forgive a player who turned up late if he offered the excuse that he had attended an Old Boys' dinner the previous night.

Hodge/Squire was probably more capable with a pint pot than either ball or bat. He marshalled his side from the vantage point of the local, the Three Horseshoes, 'tankard in hand', and his instructions to his side were 'bellowed in a most unpoetical voice'. A veritable Napoleon of the game, he emerged at crucial moments to consult the scoreboard and advise the batsmen on the appropriate tactics required, which they usually misheard or ignored.

Ballade of Soporific Absorption

Ho! Ho! Yes! Yes! it's very all well,
   You may drunk I am think, but I'll tell you I'm not,
I'm as sound as a fiddle and fit as a bell,
   And stable quite ill to see what's what,
   I under *do* stand you surprise a got

When I headed my smear with gooseberry jam;
  And I've swallowed, I grant, a beer of a lot –
But I'm not so think as you drunk I am.

Can I liquor my stand? Why, yes, like hell!
  I care not how many a tossed I've pot,
I shall stralk quite weight and not yutter an ell,
  My feet will not spalter the least little jot;
  If you knownly had one! – well I gave him a dot,
And I said to him 'Sergeant, I'll come like a lamb –
  The floor it seems like a storm in a yacht,
But I'm not so think as you drunk I am'.

For example to prove it I'll tale you a tell –
  I once knew a fellow name Apricot –
I'm sorry, I just chair over a fell –
  A trifle – this chap, on a very day hot –
  If I hadn't consumed that last whisky of tot! –
As I said now, this fellow called Abraham –
  Ah? One more? Since it's you! Just a do me will spot –
But I'm not so think as you drunk I am.

Envoi

  So, Prince, you suggest I've bolted my shot?
Well, like what you say, and soul your damn!
  I'm an upple litset by the talk you rot –
But I'm not so think as you drunk I am.

W M Thackeray

William Makepeace Thackeray – the name is as substantial as the man. He was a large figure, six feet, three inches tall, with huge appetites, driven – like his contemporary, Dickens – by an energy that seems peculiarly Victorian. He indulged himself generously during a misspent university year, giving wine parties and discovering that Cambridge ale was 'a fascinating beverage' but no aid to study. There were friends in plenty with similar tastes: 'Thirty lads round a table covered with bad sweetmeats, drinking bad wines, telling bad stories, singing bad songs over and over again.'

These friends included Edward Fitzgerald, who would win future fame for his translations of Omar Khayyam's luscious musings on wine, and a young Alfred Tennyson, wild of hair and manners. After Cambridge came the law and then the slippery slope towards Fleet Street and the company of drunken hacks – which Thackeray greatly enjoyed.

In Germany he was ostensibly studying German but took time to observe student hospitality, on which he reported: 'On breaking up, I found myself the only strictly sober man in the party although during the evening I had positively imbibed no less than six bottles of the wine … It was, after the port wine and punch of Cambridge, like so much milk and water.' He studied painting in Paris, and busied himself with other attractions that city provided: women, gambling, fine food and drink. In London he lived a highly social life. Fitzgerald remarked, 'Old Thackeray goes on his own way, writing hard for half a dozen reviews and Newspapers all the morning; dining, drinking and talking of a night.'

His stamina was as prodigious as his energy. Despite his swirling social life, he worked hard – pieces for journals such as *Punch* (notorious for riotously drunken dinners), serializations of novels that were to bring fame, such as *Vanity Fair*.

America was conquered, as Dickens had conquered it before him. Despite some health problems, the delights of the table were as powerful as ever. A Sunday breakfast at Delmonico's in New York lasted five hours and there were numerous splendid dinners. A fond family man, he kept a careful eye on his wine cellar, writing home about the visit of a guest: 'Don't give him the Liverpool Port if you ask him to dinner – that is too good for young fellows – the Balfour wine is excellent and the Kensington claret – mind, not the 40 or 60 – the young beggar doesn't know about wine yet.'

Port remained a favourite drink, one he relished alone. He happened to come across a number of rare vintage bottles in a Gray's Inn coffee house and arranged with the owner that they should be kept for his use.

> It was a rare wine. There were only a two dozen and a few bottles over, when I came to the remains of that bin, and I forthwith bargained with mine host to keep them for me. I drank every

bottle and every drop of that remainder myself. I shared never a bottle with living man; and so long as the wine lasted I slipped off to the Gray's Inn coffee house with all secrecy short of disguise, whenever I thought a dinner and a bottle by myself would do me good.

There spoke a true, passionate and unashamed lover of port.

The History of Pendennis

Now Arthur, flushed with a good deal of pride at the privilege of having the keys of the cellar, and remembering that a very few more dinners would probably take place which he and his dear friend Smirke could share, had brought up a liberal supply of claret for the company's drinking, and when the elders with little Laura left him, he and the Curate began to pass the wine very freely.

One bottle speedily yielded up the ghost, another shed more than half its blood, before the two topers had been much more than half-an-hour together – Pen, with a hollow laugh and voice, had drunk off one bumper to the falsehood of women, and had said, sardonically, that wine at any rate was a mistress who never deceived, and was sure to give a man a welcome.

Smirke gently said that he knew for his part some women who were all truth and tenderness; and casting up his eyes towards the ceiling, and heaving a sigh as if evoking some being dear and unmentionable, he took up his glass and drained it, and the rosy liquor began to suffuse his face.

Pen trolled over some verses he had been making that morning, in which he informed himself that the woman who had slighted his passion could not be worthy to win it: that he was awaking from love's mad fever, and, of course, under these circumstances, proceeded to leave her, and to quit a heartless deceiver; that a name which had one day been famous in the land, might again be heard in it; and, that though he never should be the happy and careless boy he was but a few months since, or his heart be what it had been, ere passion had filled it and grief had well-nigh killed it; that though to him personally death was as welcome as life, and that he would not hesitate to part with the latter, but for the love of one kind being whose happiness depended on his own, yet he hoped to show he was a man worthy of his race, and that one day the false one should be brought to know how great was the treasure and noble the heart which she had flung away.

Pen, we say, who was a very excitable person, rolled out these verses in his rich sweet voice, which trembled with emotion whilst our young poet spoke. He had a trick of blushing when in this excited state, and his large and honest grey eyes also exhibited proofs of a sensibility so genuine, hearty and manly, that Miss Costigan, if she had a heart, must needs have softened toward him; and very likely she was, as he said, altogether unworthy of the affection which he lavished upon her.

The sentimental Smirke was caught by the emotion which agitated his young friend. He grasped Pen's hand over the dessert dishes and wine-glasses. He said the verses were beautiful; that Pen was a poet, a great poet, and likely by Heaven's permission to run a great career in the world. 'Go on and prosper, dear Arthur,' he cried; 'the wounds under which at present you suffer are only temporary, and the very grief you endure will cleanse and strengthen your heart. I have always prophesied the greatest and brightest things of you, as soon as you have corrected some failings and weaknesses of character which at present belong to you. But you will get over these, my boy, you will get over these; and when you are famous and celebrated, as I know you will be, will you remember your old tutor and the happy early days of your youth?'

Pen swore he would: with another shake of the hand across the glasses and apricots. 'I shall never forget how kind you have been to me, Smirke,' he said. 'I don't know what I should have done without you. You are my best friend.'

'Am I *really*, Arthur?' said Smirke, looking through his spectacles; and his heart began to beat so that he thought Pen must almost hear it throbbing.

'My best friend, my friend *for ever*,' Pen said. 'God bless you, old boy,' and he drank up the last glass of the second bottle of the famous wine which his father had laid in, which his uncle had bought, which Lord Levant had imported, and which now, like a slave indifferent, was ministering pleasure to its present owner, and giving its young master delectation.

'We'll have another bottle, old boy,' Pen said; 'by Jove we will. Hurray! – claret goes for nothing. My uncle was telling me that he saw Sheridan drink five bottles at Brookes's, besides a bottle of Maraschino. This is some of the finest wine in England, he says. So it is, by Jove. There's nothing like it. *Nunc vino pellite curas – cras ingens iterabimus oeq* – fill your glass, old Smirke, a hogshead of it won't do you any harm.' And Mr Pen began to sing the drinking song out of 'Der Freischutz'.

William Wycherley

William Wycherley was a characteristic Restoration figure, a witty man of fashion, a sometime favourite at court, a soldier, a playwright and a man with a reputation.

A fine-looking man, a lover and hunter of women in the accepted manner of his age, he was introduced to court by the beautiful Duchess of Cleveland. They met when riding in opposite directions on The Mall: he saw her and turned back to take a further look and the rest is history …

In the plays we can hear the authentic voice of Restoration man: cynical, worldly, witty. Horner, the hero of *A Country Wife*, who puts it abroad that he is impotent – a ruse to further his amorous adventures – ponders on the problem of women and wine:

> I tell you, 'tis as hard to be a good fellow, a good friend, and a lover of women, as 'tis to be a good fellow, a good friend, and a lover of money. You cannot follow both, then choose your side. Wine gives you liberty, love takes it away.

He continues the thought: 'Wine gives you joy; love, grief and tortures, beside the surgeon's. Wine makes us witty; love, only sots. Wine makes us sleep; love breaks it.'

This play was a great success. Wycherley was the man of the hour for almost a full sixty minutes. Money, or rather the lack of it, was always a problem. A clandestine marriage with the Countess of Drogheda brought temporary respite but it also incurred the displeasure of the King. The Countess herself proved to be a formidable lady, keeping him on a short leash, allowing him to go to the tavern opposite only on condition that the windows stayed open so she could see what company he kept.

After his wife's death he suffered almost complete oblivion. There were years in a debtors' prison until release by James II. Noted for his splendid physique and handsome features, he remained touchingly vain, refusing to be painted without the benefit of his periwig.

On his death-bed he married a young woman, principally to pay his debts and to 'plague his damned nephew'. In death as in life, he behaved like a character in one of his own plays: while dying he received extreme unction but remembered to make his young wife swear never again to marry an old man.

The Country Wife

HORNER Well, a pox on love and wenching! Women serve but to keep a man from better company; though I can't enjoy them, I shall you the more. Good fellowship and friendship are lasting, rational, and manly pleasures.

HARCOURT For all that, give me some of those pleasures you call effeminate too; they help to relish one another.

HORNER They disturb one another.

HARCOURT No, mistresses are like books. If you pore upen them too much, they doze you and make you unfit for company; but if used discreetly you are the fitter for conversation by 'em.

DORILAND A mistress should be like a little country retreat near the town, not to dwell in constantly, but only for a night and away, to taste the town the better when a man returns.

HORNER I tell you, 'tis as hard to be a good fellow, a good friend, and a lover of women, as 'tis to be a good fellow, a good friend, and a lover of money. You cannot follow both, then choose your side. Wine gives you liberty, love takes it away.

DORILANT Gad, he's in the right on't.

HORNER Wine gives you joy; love, grief and tortures, besides the surgeon's. Wine makes us witty; love, only sots. Wine makes us sleep; love breaks it.

DORILANT By the world, he has reason, Harcourt.

HORNER Wine makes—

DORILAND Ay, wine makes us – makes us princes; love makes us beggars, poor rogues, egad – and wine—

HORNER I grant it; love will still be uppermost.

HORNER Come, for my part I will have only those glorious, manly pleasures of being very drunk and very slovenly.

Enter BOY

BOY Mr. Sparkish is below, sir.

HARCOURT What, my dear friend! A rogue that is fond of me only, I think, for abusing him.

DORILANT No, he can no more think the men laugh at him than that women jilt him, his opinion of himself is so good.

HORNER Well, there's another pleasure by drinking I thought not of; I shall lose his acquaintance, because he cannot drink; and you know 'tis a very hard thing to be rid of him, for he's one of those nauseous offerers at wit, who, like the worst fiddlers, run themselves into all companies …

DORILANT But I would no more sup with women, unless I could lie with 'em, than sup with a rich coxcomb, unless I could cheat him.

HORNER Yes, I have known thee sup with a fool for his drinking; if he could set out your hand that way only, you were satisfied, and if he were a wine-swallowing mouth 'twas enough.

HARCOURT Yes, a man drinks often with a fool, as he tosses with a marker, only to keep his hand in ure. But do the ladies drink?

HORNER Yes, sir, and I shall have the pleasure at least of laying 'em flat with a bottle, and bring as much scandal that way upon 'em as formerly t'other.

HARCOURT Perhaps you may prove as weak a brother amongst 'em that way as t'other.

DORILAND Foh! drinking with women is as unnatural as scolding with 'em; but 'tis a pleasure of decayed fornicators, and the basest way of quenching love.

HARCOURT Nay, 'tis drowning love instead of quenching it. But leave us for civil women too!

DORILAND Ay, when he can't be the better for 'em. We hardly pardon a man that leaves his friend for a wench, and that's a pretty lawful call.

HORNER Faith, I would not leave you for 'em, if they would not drink.

DORILAND Who would disappoint his company at Lewis's for a gossiping?

HARCOURT Foh! Wine and women, good apart, together as nauseous as sack and sugar. But hark you, sir, before you go, a little of your advice; an old maimed general, when unfit for action, is fittest for counsel. I have other designs upon women than eating and drinking with them. I am in love with Sparkish's mistress, whom he is to marry tomorrow. Now how shall I get her?

William Shakespeare

There is, of course, no direct evidence about what William Shakespeare favoured in the matter of drink, just as there is no direct evidence about anything else he favoured in life. The best known of English writers, and easily the most quoted, he remains an enigma.

There is, however, circumstantial evidence about what he drank in his plays. Take, for example, the case of Sack, which is the wine most mentioned in his works. Sack, Sherry-Sack or Canary was an amber-coloured wine, usually dry but occasionally sweetened with sugar or honey, that was hugely popular in Elizabethan times.

It is the subject of extravagant praise by Falstaff in *Henry IV, part II*. But this wine was unknown in England during the reigns of Henry IV and Henry V – it is first mentioned in 1532. The historical Falstaff could never have known the wine and it is reasonable to assume that the paean of praise for the drink comes from the direct experience of none other than Will Shakespeare.

The plays are peppered with references to it. Falstaff calls for it endlessly in *Henry IV*, *part II*, and in *The Merry Wives of Windsor*. It is no surprise that the fat knight is chided by Prince Hal in the former play: 'Thou art so fat-witted with drinking old Sack.'

Medical opinion seemed to bear out Prince Hal's comments, certainly as far as Falstaff was concerned. William Vaughan in 1600 considered that: 'Sacke doth make men fat and foggy, and therefore not to be taken by young men. Being drunk before supper with store of sugar, it provoketh appetite, comforteth the spirits marvellously, and concocteth raw humours.'

This same authority recommended a wine, mentioned often in Shakespeare's plays, called Bastard. It was a sweet wine, probably like the modern Beaumes-des-Venise, from France. He advised that 'these kindes of wines are onely for married folkes, because they strengthen the backe'.

Wine, with beer, was the staple drink of the Elizabethan age; ale at breakfast and wine thereafter was the rule. Wine was cheap and readily available: fourpence a gallon for wine a year or less old. The wines mentioned in *The Taming of The Shrew*, *The Merry Wives of Windsor*, *A Midsummer Night's Dream*, and other plays, were the wines drunk in the inns of London. The selection for the wine buff in those days was quite as good as that available today, with the exception of wines from the New World which, happily perhaps, did not exist.

Wine was shipped from France: claret and graves from Bordeaux and from La Rochelle, Orleans and Anjou. Apart from Sack – the best came from Jerez – Spain provided wines from Malaga, Alicante and the Canary islands. Madeira provided Malmsey, a barrel of which, according to Shakespeare, was the final glorious resting place of the Duke of Clarence.

Henry IV, part II

> A good Sherris-Sack hath a two-fold operation in it: it ascends me into the Braine, dryes me there all the foolish, and dull, and cruddie Vapours, which enuiron it: makes it apprehensiue, quicke, for getiue, full of nimble, fierie, and delectable shapes; which deliuer'd o're to the Voyce, the Tongue, which is the Birth, becomes excellent Wit. The second propertie of your excellent Sherris, is, the warming of the Blood: which before (cold, and setled) left the Liuer white, and pale; which is the Badge of Pusillanimitie, and Cowardize; but the Sherris warmes it, and makes it course from the inwards, to the parts extremes: it illuminateth the Face, which (as a Beacon) gives warning to all the rest of this litt kingdome (Man) to Arme: and then the Vitall Commoners and in-land pettie Spirits, must me all to their Captaine, the Heart; who great, and pufft up with his Retinue, doth any Deed of Courage: and this Valour comes of Sherris. So, that skill in the Weapon is nothing, without Sack (for that sets it a-worke:) and Learning a meere Hoord of Gold, kept by a Devill, till Sack commences it, and sets it in act, and use. Hereof comes it, that Prince *Harry* is valiant: for the cold blood hee did naturally inherite of his Father, hee hath, like leane, stirrill, and bare Land, manured, husbanded, and

> tyll'd, with excellent endeauour of drinking good, and good store of fertile Sherris, that hee is become very hot and valiant. If I had a thousand Sonnes, the first Principle I would teach them, should be to forsweare thinne Potations, and to addict themselves to Sack …

R S Surtees

Surtees created one of the best-known characters in fiction, Mr Jorrocks, who is known by many who have never opened one of his books for a few phrases: 'Come hup, I say, you hughly beast!' and 'Hellish dark and smells of cheese.'

R S Surtees was a country gentleman from Northumberland, a hunting man, a magistrate, Lord Lieutenant of the county, a man who was worlds away from that of his famous fat, hard-drinking, cussing Cockney grocer. The phrase Dickensian is often used in referring to Jorrocks, who was born some five years before Dickens created the immortal Mr Pickwick.

Surtees provided hospitality on a grand scale. Nimrod, the famous writer on hunting of the period, was deeply impressed by his reception:

> He being the most religious observer of the remains of ancient times, in the unbounded hospitality of his house and table – one who it might be imagined had he himself existed in those ancient times when men had high notions of the rights of hospitality, and not merely the rules of civility: when, as Homer says, strangers were received as guests from heaven …

Pausing for breath, Nimrod goes on to say that he drank more claret in the few days he stayed at Surtees' country estate 'than I had in that space of time for many a long day before.'

Surtees was a taciturn man in later life, dignified and respectable, but he had enjoyed his youth. He was especially fond of Brighton when the resort still had its Regency character and was noted for balls, dances and dinners. He also ran a pack of foxhounds near Boulogne. At one hunt dinner the owner of the local inn was carried home on a stretcher some time after midnight.

Surtees claimed to prefer dinner at his club with a leisurely bottle of wine but Mr Jorrocks had very different tastes on his excursions to London:

> Dinner time comes, and Lord Cut and Shuffle has the rich man on the box of his drag – four spankin' bays, tigers be'ind, friends on the roof, gals inside. Away they bowl to Greenwich – best room, dinner two guineas a 'ead, iced fizzy – fish of all sorts. Hopera – time for ballet – squizzin' glass – gauze petticoats – or hup Windmill Street to the sparklin' French Casino or down heast to the British 'bomination of a dingy underground kidney shop/ These at length bein' swept out and closed, away they go to some sham billiard room of a fortified gamblin' 'ouse, with scouts on watch where they have some cureasore to digest the kidneys – iced champagne to correct the cureasore – lobster salad to keep the champagne company.

Handley Cross

About nine, Betsey brought the supper-tray, and Jorrocks would treat Pigg to a glass of brandy and water. One glass led to another, and they had a strong talk about hunting. They drank each other's healths, then the healths of the hounds.

'I'll give you old Priestess's goo 'ealth!' exclaimed Mr Jorrocks, holding up his glass. 'Fine old bitch, with her tan eyebrows – thinks I never saw a better 'ound – wise as a Christian!' Pigg proposed Manager. Mr Jorrocks gave Rummager. Pigg gave Dexterous; and they drank Mercury, and Affable, and Crowner, and Lousey, and Mountebank, and Milliner – almost all the pack in short.

The fire began to hiss, and Mr Jorrocks felt confident his prophecy was about to be fulfilled.

'Look out of the winder, James, and see wot sort of a night it is,' said he to Pigg, giving the log a stir to ascertain that the hiss didn't proceed from any dampness in the wood.

James staggered up, and after a momentary grope about the room – for they were sitting without candles – exclaimed 'Hellish dark and smells of cheese!'

'*Smells o' cheese*!' repeated Mr Jorrocks, looking round; 'vy man, you've got your nob in the cupboard – this is the vinder,' going to the other corner, and opening some shutters painted like the cupboard-door, and throwing up the sash.

Oscar Wilde

Oscar Wilde's list of accomplishments is well known. He was a poet, playwright, critic, talker and wit. To this list can be added another, less expected distinction: drinker.

At the height of his fame he was the most sought-after guest in London, the ultimate distinction for any hostess of ambition. He charmed all who met him in Society, holding them spellbound in a flow of talk so bewitching, it was said, that no one could ever remember a word of it afterwards.

He also drank mightily on these occasions but was, astonishingly, never known to be drunk. Despite his languid posturing and effeminate mannerisms, he had the constitution (and something of the build) of a carthorse as well as a head of iron.

'I have discovered,' he said, 'that alcohol, taken in sufficient quantity, produces all the effects of drunkenness.' There is also some evidence in his works that he was something of a connoisseur of wine. For example, in *The Importance of Being Earnest*, Jack complains that Algernon had drunk 'an entire pint bottle of my Perrier-Jouet '89, a wine I was specially reserving for myself'. Jack's chagrin is understandable when we learn – according to that unimpeachable authority, Michael Broadbent – that 1889 was, indeed, an outstanding vintage for champagne. Burgundy, especially Chambertin, is also mentioned.

Wilde was a late-night person throughout his life, partly because he seldom rose until late in the morning. During the performances of his plays he would be at the bar, buying rounds of drinks for friends, and after the show drinking hot port with friends such as Beerbohm and Beardsley at pubs, such as The Crown off Charing Cross Road, until 12.30 am before going on for further sustenance.

After his disgrace and resulting imprisonment, Wilde resumed his drinking habits, particularly absinthe. Typically, he said, he was attracted by the colour. 'Absinthe has a wonderful colour, green. A glass of absinthe is as poetical as anything in the world. What difference is there between a glass of absinthe and a sunset?' This difference may not be clear to anyone who has been drinking absinthe.

Even in this period he was never observed behaving in a drunken fashion. Although described as a 'three decanter man' and having a passion for absinthe for which 'he would have hobnobbed with a porter', he was still the essential Oscar in that his wit remained intact. He responded to criticism from a fellow poet for being drunk: '*Il faut accepter la personalite comme elle est. Il ne faut jamais regretter qu'un poete est saoul, il faut regretter que les soulards ne soient pas toujours poetes.*' ('Personality must be accepted for what it is. One must not regret that a poet is drunk but that drunks are not always poets.')

More down-to-earth was his remark: '*Qu'importe le verre, pouvou qu'on ait l'ivress.*' ('The glass doesn't matter, provided one has the drunkenneness.').

The Picture of Dorian Gray

Lord Henry Wootton: 'I quite sympathize with the rage of the English democracy against what they call the vices of the upper orders. The masses feel that drunkenness, stupidity and immorality should be their own special property, and that if any one of us makes an ass of himself he is poaching on their preserves.'

'Beer, The Bible, and the seven deadly virtues have made our England what she is.'

'He played with the idea, and grew wilful; tossed it into the air and transformed it; let it escape and recaptured it; made it iridescent with fancy, and winged it with paradox, The praise of folly, as he went on, soared into a philosophy, and Philosophy herself became young, and catching the mad music of Pleasure, wearing, one might fancy, her wine-stained robe and wreath of ivy, danced like a Bacchante over the hills of life, and mocked the slow Silenus for being sober. Facts fled before her light frightened forest things. Her white feet trod the huge press at which wise Omar sits, till the seething grape-juice rose round her bare limbs in waves of purple bubbles, or crawled in red foam over the vat's black, dripping, sloping sides.'

*P*ARTY *T*IME

One must get drunk but in good Company.
That is to say, with good Friends,
people of Wit, Honour and good Humour,
and where there is good Wine.

eighteenth-century pamphlet

L DA PONTE	'Champagne Aria'
F S FITZGERALD	*Tender Is The Night*
PETRONIUS	*Satyricon*
PLATO	*Symposium*
J RHYS	*Let Them Call it Jazz*
J STEINBECK	*Cannery Row*

Lorenzo Da Ponte

Da Ponte is one of the few librettists to have escaped the anonymity of his profession. His life – an almost unbelievable mix of intrigue, misunderstandings, love affairs, great success, miserable failure and hopeless debts – would have made an excellent subject for an opera, and only he would have been capable of doing justice to it.

He is best remembered for the three great libretti he wrote for Mozzart (as he always called him): *Così fan tutte*, *Don Giovanni*, and *Le Nozze di Figaro* – although he wrote some fifty libretti for many composers.

He shared some similarities with Don Giovanni, not only in a taste for amorous dissipation, but in the joyful appetite for life as expressed in the 'Champagne Aria' sung by the eponymous hero of that opera. The character, in fact, was based on Casanova, a fellow Venetian and lifelong friend.

Da Ponte was a remarkably fluent writer, although he may have exaggerated this facility in the following quotation concerning how he set about writing three libretti for three composers at the same time: 'I went to my desk and stayed for twelve hours without a break. A bottle of Tokay on my right, the ink-well in the middle and a box of Seville snuff on the left.' Whenever he required anything he rang a bell for the daughter of the house, 'A beautiful young girl of sixteen (whom I would have liked to love simply as a daughter but …)'. Da Ponte describes his progress thus:

> On the first day. Meanwhile, between the Tokay, the snuff, the coffee, the bell and my young muse, I wrote the first two scenes of *Don Giovanni*, two of *L'Arbore di Diana* and more than half the first act of *Tatar* …

Da Ponte's burst of creativity could be attributed to the powers of the legendary wine of Hungary, Tokay, for it was this wine that moved Voltaire to write: 'This wine invigorates every fibre of the brain and brings forth an enchanting sparkle of wit and good cheer from the depths of the soul.'

Mozart was an equally fluent composer, of course, but did not always enjoy such delightful circumstances for his work. It was not a great penance, however, when he was tricked into being led into a room and locked in so he would complete the overture for *Don Giovanni* which was due to be performed. A contemporary described how two bottles of wine and food were tied to long poles and handed up to Mozart. Da Ponte, who was part of the plot, showed a practical appreciation of the situation, 'appearing with a rake to which an article was attached which was as necessary as it was unaesthetic'.

'You'll need this, too. Take it, divine maestro …'

'A pity it's empty,' Mozart said, 'otherwise it would be the worse for you.'

Da Ponte's career as a librettist took him on many adventures in Vienna and London but he spent the last thirty years of his life in America, involved in all kinds of enterprise, including selling provisions, teaching Italian and becoming a university professor. It was from there that he wrote: 'though seventythree years have passed, they don't weigh very heavily yet … I still eat well, drink well, sleep peacefully and – which amazes people – spend six, eight, ten and sometimes twelve hours a day working and writing poetry, too.'

In fact, he lived until he was nearly 90, still ardent in his self-appointed aim of promoting Italian opera and, indeed, other important aspects of Italian life in America. He advised visitors from Italy to bring Italian vine roots, wine from Florence, maraschino, pasta and Parmesan to the New World.

Champagne Aria

Whilst from wine
Their heads are heated,
A great party
Let there be prepared!

If in the market place you find
Some pretty girls
These too try
To bring along with you.

Without any set order,
Let the dancing be,
Some the minuet,
Some the 'follia'
Some the allemande,
You'll make dance.

And I meanwhile,
On the other hand,
With this one and that one
Want to flirt!

Oh, my little list
Tomorrow morning,
By half a score,
You have to augment.

F Scott Fitzgerald

Scott Fitzgerald was the poet of the Jazz Age, a time when America was on the spree, swept up in the giddy pursuit of a golden goal called fun. Life was one long party and everybody was invited. The bands played, everybody danced and everybody, but everybody, drank. Prohibition added to the spice of life with bootleg booze, gangsters and speak-easies.

Fitzgerald not only wrote about this world, he embodied it. He was young, handsome and – above all – successful. He and Zelda were the stars of the show, leading players in a dazzling, romantic drama.

It's all there in his first novel, *This Side of Paradise*, and in the stream of stories that appeared in a clutch of popular magazines and for which Fitzgerald was highly paid. He worked like a demon to sustain his lifestyle, earning large sums but spending even larger amounts, going on the wagon at one point to churn out eleven stories in six months.

His teetotalling did not last long. He lived, as he said, in 'a blaze of work and liquor', producing more stories and what is probably his finest book, *The Great Gatsby*.

F. Scott Fitzgerald

The pursuit of pleasure took Fitzgerald and Zelda further afield, to Paris, and Antibes in the South of France. Hemingway met him in Paris and they became friends over a couple of bottles of champagne. Hemingway described his experiences of Fitzgerald in *A Moveable Feast*, a book of recollections about people he had met in Paris but which, perhaps inadvertently, concentrates on the author's sterling qualities rather than those of anyone else. He describes how Fitzgerald passed out on what Hemingway obviously thinks of as a pitifully small amount of drink but included a number of bottles of Maçon wine and several double whiskies. Despite this testimony from the hard-headed and, we are given to understand, apparently infallible author (Hemingway also describes how he reassured Fitzgerald about the size of his penis) it is true that Fitzgerald was becoming more dependent on alcohol and was well on the way to becoming an alcoholic. Nevertheless, he continued to work while he drank during the mental deterioration of Zelda, who finally lived out her years in a sanatorium. Fitzgerald survived stints in Hollywood in addition to the work on his own books.

He died, pitifully young, at 44. There is no doubt that Scott Fitzgerald's life was dominated by drinking, and that he was eventually ruined by it. But this fate was somehow inescapable, given his character and the mood of the period he lived in. Drink was part of the world he captured so perfectly, so vividly, particularly in *The Great Gatsby* and Fitzgerald's life and death have echoes of one of his fictional characters from the Jazz Age.

Tender is the Night

The party that night moved with the speed of a slapstick comedy. They were twelve, they were sixteen, they were quartets in separate motors bound on a quick odyssey over Paris. Everything had been foreseen. People joined them as if by magic, accompanied them as specialists, almost guides, through a phase of the evening, dropped out and were succeeded by other people, so that it appeared as if the freshness of each one had been husbanded for them all day. Rosemary appreciated how different it was from any party in Hollywood, no matter how splendid in scale. There was, among many diversions, the car of the Shah of Persia. Where Dick had commandeered this vehicle, what bribery was employed, these were facts of irrelevance. Rosemary accepted it as merely a new facet of the fabulous, which for two years had filled her life. The car had been built on a special chassis in America. Its wheels were of silver, so was the radiator. The inside of the body was inlaid with innumerable brilliants, which would be replaced with true gems by the court jeweller when the car arrived in Teheran the following week. There was only one real seat in the back, because the Shah must ride alone, so they took turns riding in it and sitting on the marten fur that covered the floor …

The time she laughed most was later, when six of them, the best of them, noblest relics of the evening, stood in the dusky front lobby of the Ritz telling the night concierge that General Pershing was outside and wanted caviar and champagne. 'He brooks no delay. Every man, every gun is at his service.' Frantic waiters emerged from nowhere, a table was set in the lobby, and Abe came in representing General Pershing while they stood up and mumbled frequent fragments of war songs at him. In the waiters' injured reaction to this anti-climax they found themselves neglected, so they built a waiter trap – a huge and fantastic device constructed of all the furniture in the lobby and functioning like one of the bizarre machines of a Goldberg cartoon …

Later Rosemary and the Norths and a manufacturer of dolls' voices from Newark and the ubiquitous Collis and a big splendidly-dressed oil Indian named George T. Horse-protection were riding along on top of thousands of carrots in a market wagon. The earth in the carrot beards was fragrant and sweet in the darkness, and Rosemary was so high up in the load that she could hardly see the others in the long shadow between infrequent street lamps. Their voices came from far off, as if they were having experiences different from hers, different and far away, for she was with Dick in her heart, sorry she had come with the Norths, wishing she was at the hotel and Dick asleep across the hall, or that he was here beside her with the warm darkness streaming down.

'Don't come up,' she called to Collis, 'the carrots will all roll.' She threw one at Abe, who was sitting beside the driver, stiffly like an old man …

Later she was homeward bound at last in broad daylight, with the pigeons already breaking over Saint-Sulpice. All of them began to laugh spontaneously, because they knew it was still last night while the people in the streets had the delusion that it was bright hot morning.

'At last I've been on a wild party,' thought Rosemary, 'but it's no fun when Dick isn't here.'

She felt a little betrayed and sad, but presently a moving object came into sight. It was a huge horse-chestnut tree in full bloom bound for the Champs-Elysées, strapped now into a long truck and simply shaking with laughter – like a lovely person in an undignified position yet confident none the less of being lovely. Looking at it with satisfaction, Rosemary identified herself with it, and laughed cheerfully with it, and everything all at once seemed gorgeous.

Petronius

In Trimalchio, the boozy, vulgar self-made man who appears in the *Satyricon*, the Latin poet Petronius created one of the great monsters of fiction. He is loud, lewd, utterly impossible and totally believable.

The dinner party given by Trimalchio, as described by Petronius, is as different from that depicted by Plato in the *Symposium* as it is possible to be. Where Plato's work is stately in tone, moralistic in intention, Petronius writes in idiomatic style with what seems to be the single intention of entertaining his reader.

The *Satyricon* is a satire on popular romances of the time in which pure heroes and heroines overcame all manner of obstacles to live happily ever after. In the *Satyricon* the hero and heroine are replaced by a string of disreputable characters who have a series of fantastic adventures, usually involving various complicated sexual practices.

Petronius knew all about and doubtless participated in the decadent life of Rome. For a time he was a favourite at the court of Nero and acted as a sort of master of revels. Nero's debauchery was matched by a general decline of morals in Rome. The historian Tacitus reported that 'every form of immorality competed for attention, and no chastity, modesty or vestige of decency could survive'. The people devoted their lives, another historian remarked, to drink, gambling, brothels, shows and pleasure in general.

In such circumstances, drunkenness was a minor aberration, although Roman-style drinking could be spectacular, again as reported by Tacitus, this time on the 'extravagances' of Messalina, wife of Claudius.

> It was full autumn; and she was performing in her grounds a mimic grape-harvest. Presses were working, vats overflowing, surrounded by women capering in skins like sacrifices or frenzied Maenads. She herself, hair streaming, brandished a Bacchic wand.

When Petronius fell from Nero's favour he killed himself by bleeding slowly to death, a form of suicide much favoured by Romans. He was a brave man, talking, and even joking, as his life ebbed away. As a final act he sent Nero a full list of his most private debaucheries rather than the usual homage to the emperor, which was the expected form of behaviour in such cases.

Satyricon

> 'A word in your ears: if you own a penny, you're worth a penny. A man's as good as his income. Have a long look in my direction, fables come true, a frog yesterday, a fairy prince today, and now I think of it Stichus, get out the shroud I'm going to be carried out in; and some of the ointment too, while you're about it, and just a moistening of that vintage they'll be washing my corpse down with.'
>
> Stichus hurried off and came back into the dining-room laden with the white winding-sheet and the gown of office for the funeral. Trimalchio bade us feel them and see the class of wool they were woven of. Then with a grim laugh, 'Take good care, Stichus,' he said, 'that no mice or moths riddle them, or I'll roast you alive, you know. I mean to be carried out in state so that all the crowd will cheer and say a blessing.'
>
> And he uncorked the flask of the ointment and anointed us all with it, saying, 'I hope you'll find the stuff as fragrant when I'm dead as I do now.'
>
> And not content with that, he had a bowl filled with the wine, and said, 'Now you must imagine to yourselves you're guests at my wake.'
>
> The whole affair was growing intolerable. Trimalchio, who by this time was rolling drunk, belched out a summons for yet another turn, a set of trumpeters. When they arrived, he propped

himself up on a mound of cushions and stretched his body out rigidly on its death-bed. 'Pretend I'm dead,' he said, 'go on, say what a fine fellow I was.'

The trumpeters blared out into a funeral march. One of the troupe, a slave of the undertaker who was the most respectable member of the party, blurted out such a terrific bray that the whole neighbourhood was aroused, and the patrol of the local watch thought Trimalchio's house must have caught fire. They rushed up, broke in the front door, and started to do their duty of causing a turmoil with axes and buckets of water. The opportunity was too good to miss; we said good-bye to Agamemnon, and went off helter-skelter as though we were really escaping from a burning house.

Plato

The dinner party in 416 BC described by Plato in his *Symposium* was a pretty sober, even dull affair, until the arrival of Alcibiades towards the end. Socrates and Aristophanes were among the guests, each of whom gave a speech on the subject of love, which was a departure from the usual entertainment by female dancers and flute-girls.

The dinner party described in this dramatic dialogue could well have been a real event, as occasions of this kind were popular among upper-class gentlemen of Athens at the time. Drinking parties were immensely popular and regularly held, although they were often much more indecorous affairs when attended by less high-minded guests.

The vine had been widely cultivated in Athens since time immemorial. Centuries before Plato, Homer had made many references to it in the *Odyssey*: 'the grapes are drying in the sun, while others are gathered or being trodden. And on the foremost rows hang unripe bunches that have just cast their blossom or show the first faint tinge of purple.' Then there is Odysseus recalling a scene where 'my mother, who generally sits in the firelight by the hearth, weaving yarn stained with sea-purple, and forming a delightful picture, with her chair against a pillar, and her maids sitting behind. My father's throne is close to hers, and there he sits drinking his wine like a god.'

Wine was abundant, as a day-to-day drink and as an ingredient in the religious cults of Dionysus, the god of wine. The wine drunk by the guests at Plato's dinner party would not have been Athenian *vin ordinaire* but old wine, sweet and strong. The finest and oldest wines were usually watered down. The amounts of water varied considerably, half and half was considered normal, some thought three parts water to one of wine. Many wines were adulterated, sometimes with honey but also with resin, which is still used in Greek wine, as thousands of modern visitors will remember with pleasure or repugnance. At drinking parties the host, or a nominated person, would act as a presiding authority and decide how strong the wine should be – a decision often influenced by the urging of fellow guests, the more seasoned drinkers calling for stronger wine.

Plato was sober in all things but took a relaxed view about drinking. He seems to have believed, with the later Romans, that drinking was a true revelation of character: 'no experiment is less costly, and none shall bear fruit more surely and more quickly, if we wish to test the different characters of men, to judge them, and to be guided in the art of making them better, than to know them in the "truth of the drunk".'

Socrates had a legendary reputation as a drinker because he was able to drink enormous quantities without showing the least sign of insobriety. From the arrival of Alcibiades, which is described below, the standard of behaviour and discourse degenerated as the night went on. More revellers arrived to take part in drinking but gradually all fell asleep, overcome by wine. As dawn appeared, only Socrates was left, as rational, sober and loquacious (and irritating, perhaps) as when he arrived.

Symposium

Suddenly they heard a loud knocking at the door of the vestibule, and a clamour as of revellers, attended by a flute-player.

'Go, boy,' said Agathon, 'and see who is there: if they are any of friends, call them in; if not, say that we have already done drinking.'

A minute afterwards, they heard the voice of Alcibiades in the vestibule excessively drunk and roaring out: 'Where is Agathon? Lead me to Agathon!'

The flute-player, and some of his companions then led him in, and placed him against the door-post, crowned with a thick crown of ivy and violets and having a quantity of fillets on his head.

'My friends,' he cried out, 'hail! I am excessively drunk already, but I'll drink with you, if you will. If not, we will go away after having crowned Agathon, for which purpose I came. I assure you that I could not come yesterday, but I am now here with these fillets round my temples that from my own head I may crown him who, with your leave, is the most beautiful and wisest of men. Are you laughing at me because I am drunk? Ay, I know what I say is true, whether you laugh or not. But tell me at once whether I shall come in, or no. Will you drink with me?'

Agathon and the whole party desired him to come in, and recline among them; so he came in, led by his companions. He then unbound his fillets that he might crown Agathon, and though Socrates was just before his eyes he did not see him, but sat down by Agathon, between Socrates and him, for Socrates moved out of the way to make room for him. When he sat down, he embraced Agathon and crowned him, and Agathon desired the slaves to untie his sandals, that he might make a third, and recline on the same couch.

'By all means,' said Alcibiades, 'but what third companion have we here?' And at the same time turning round and seeing Socrates, he leaped up and cried out:

'O Hercules! what have we here? You, Socrates, lying in ambush for me wherever I go! and meeting me just as you always do when I least expected to see you! ...' Saying this, he took the fillets, and having bound the head of Socrates, and again having reclined, said: 'Come, my friends you seem to be sober enough. You must not flinch, but drink, for that was your agreement with me before I came in. I choose as president, until you have drunk enough – myself. Come, Agathon, if you have got a great goblet, fetch it out. But no matter, the wine-cooler will do: bring it, boy!'

Jean Rhys

Drinking is a common activity among the characters in the stories of Jean Rhys, as common as sex, and perhaps more satisfying. They drink in a subdued, fatalistic way: there is nothing violent in their drinking, no exuberance or wild excess, only a faint changing of behaviour.

Drink was a necessary part of Jean Rhys, as an individual and as a writer. Her essentially autobiographical stories touch on its role in her life: poor and lonely, often desperately disappointed in London and Paris, sustained and supported by drinking. In *Voyage in the Dark*, *Quarter* and *On Leaving Mr Mackenzie*, fear and loneliness are eased by drink.

Carole Angier, in her book on Jean Rhys, says she had to drink to write and she had to drink to live. She sometimes drank two bottles of wine a day when writing. She was utterly candid in her letters, about getting tight, needing to drink to get on with her work, tippling on vodka while writing letters, or on whisky provided by a sympathetic local parson.

Unfortunately, Jean Rhys did not take drink as placidly as most of her characters. She flew into violent rages when drunk, overwhelmed by old grievances, transformed from her usually sweet temperament, alienating all but her oldest and most compassionate friends.

When writing her classic *Wide Sargasso Sea* she drank to get herself in the mood: 'one day drunk, two days hung-over, regular as clockwork'. Yet the work was completed and was a triumph, against all the odds, against physical weakness brought about by age and heavy drinking. Frail, difficult, self-destructive, there was something indomitable about her and something heroic in her struggle to live and to write. It was a struggle that finally ended just short of her 89th birthday in rural Devon.

Let Them Call it Jazz

… and I get the habit of buying a bottle of wine most evenings, for I don't like whisky and the rum here no good. It don't even *taste* like rum. You wonder what they do to it.

After I drink a glass or two I can sing and when I sing all the misery goes from my heart. Sometimes I make up songs but next morning I forget them, so other times I sing the old ones like 'Tantalizin', or 'Don't Trouble Me Now'.

I think I go but I don't go. Instead I wait for the evening and the wine and that's all. Everywhere else I live – well, it doesn't matter to me, but this house is different – empty and no noise and full of shadows, so that sometimes you ask yourself what make all those shadows in an empty room.

I eat in the kitchen, then I clean up everything and have a bath for coolness. Afterwards I lean my elbows on the windowsill and look at the garden. Red and blue flowers mix up with the weeds and there are five–six apple trees. But the fruit drop and lie in the grass, so sour nobody want it. At the back, near the wall, is a bigger tree – this garden certainly take up a lot of room, perhaps that's why they want to pull the place down.

Not much rain all the summer, but not much sunshine either. More of a glare. The grass get brown and dry, the weeds grow tall, the leaves on the trees hang down. Only the red flowers – the poppies – stand up to that light, everything else look weary.

I don't trouble about money, but what with wine and shillings for the slot-meters, it go quickly; so I don't waste much on food. In the evening I walk outside – not by the apple trees but near the street – it's not so lonely.

There's no wall here and I can see the woman next door looking at me over the hedge. At first I say good evening, but she turn away her head, so afterwards I don't speak. A man is often with her, he wear a straw hat with a black ribbon and goldrim spectacles. His suit hang on him like it's too big. He's the husband it seems and he stare at me worse than his wife – he stare as if I'm wild animal let loose. Once I laugh in his face because why these people have to be like that? I don't bother them. In the end I get that I don't even give them one single glance. I have plenty other things to worry about.

To show you how I felt. I don't remember exactly. But I believe it's the second Saturday after I come that when I'm at the window just before I go for my wine I feel somebody's hand on my shoulder and it's Mr Sims. He must walk very quiet because I don't know a thing till he touch me.

He says hullo, then he tells me I've got terrible thin, do I ever eat. I say of course I eat but he goes on that it doesn't suit me at all to be so thin and he'll buy some food in the village. (That's the way he talk. There's no village here. You don't get away from London so quick.)

It don't seem to me he look very well himself, but I just say bring a drink instead, as I am not hungry.

He come back with three bottles – vermouth, gin and red wine.

Then he ask if the little devil who was here last smash all the glasses and I tell him she smash some. I find the pieces. But not all. 'You fight with her, eh?'

John Steinbeck

John Steinbeck belongs to that group of American writers who seemed to roll off some literary production line as smoothly as the latest Ford. Hemingway, Faulkner, Fitzgerald: all were variations on the standard model of Great American Novelist.

These writers shared a propensity for excess: in terms of sales, in personal life – wives, lovers – and in drinking. Steinbeck was a boozer but not, it would seem, an alcoholic. His life, like that of many authors of his generation, was fuelled by alcohol. It is a preoccupation of many of his characters, the denizens of *Cannery Row*, for example, and *Tortilla Flat*. Doc is based on a real character, Ed Ricketts, a marine biologist, equally capable of drinking large quantities of alcohol, who was a close friend.

Steinbeck was a young man in the rip-roaring years of Prohibition and, like every other right-thinking American, drank his share – and perhaps more – of bootleg gin and whiskey. When funds were short or supplies unavailable, he made his own wine. The red, a friend recalled, was 'foul but strong' and he also made an alarming-sounding fig wine. 'We make beer, much beer, and it is both cheap and pleasant,' he wrote from California to a friend in the east.

Like Hemingway, with whom he is often – and unfavourably – compared as a writer, Steinbeck was a husky outdoor type. While working at a fish hatchery, the foreman found him in his bunk with a bottle of bootleg gin, shooting holes in the ceiling. But he had a softer centre. When writing his first book, *Cup of Gold*, he confessed to 'being drunk for three days, a horrible period wherein I hurled duty taunts at my spirit'.

'There was a wild streak in John,' recalled Burgess Meredith, the actor and a good friend. 'When he got going – usually after a few shots of whiskey or a quantity of beer – you couldn't keep him down.'

Such books as *Of Mice and Men* and *The Grapes of Wrath* made Steinbeck a wealthy man. He was an international figure, hobnobbing with statesmen, and winning the Nobel Prize.

Drinking did not appear to affect his creativity or his enormous output. *The Grapes of Wrath*, all 200,000 words of it, was written in some six months. This mammoth effort was not achieved in monastic denial: there were days when too much champagne was drunk, others when it was too much whiskey. But nothing could stop the progress of what proved to be a classic American novel.

Cannery Row

In mid-morning the Model T truck rolled triumphantly home to Cannery Row and hopped the gutter and creaked up through the weeds to its place behind Lee Chong's. The boys blocked up the front wheels, drained what petrol was left into a five-gallon can, took their frogs, and went wearily home to the Palace Flophouse. Then Mack made a ceremonious visit to Lee Chong while the boys got a fire going in the big stove. Mack thanked Lee with dignity for lending the truck. He spoke of the great success of the trip, of the hundreds of frogs taken. Lee smiled shyly and waited for the inevitable.

'We're in the chips,' Mack said enthusiastically, 'Doc pays us a nickel a frog and we got about a thousand.'

Lee nodded. The price was standard. Everybody knew that.

'Doc's away,' said Mack. 'Jesus, is he gonna be happy when he sees all them frogs.'

Lee nodded again. He knew Doc was away and he also knew where the conversation was going.

'Say, by the way,' said Mack as though he had just thought of it. 'We're a little bit short right now ...' He managed to make it sound like a very unusual situation.

'No whisky,' said Lee Chong, and he smiled.

Mack was outraged. 'What would we want whisky for? Why, we got a gallon of the finest whisky you ever laid a lip over – a whole full God-damned-running over gallon. By the way,' he continued, 'I and the boys would like to have you just step up for a snort with us. They told me to ask you.'

In spite of himself Lee smiled with pleasure. They wouldn't offer it if they didn't have it.

'No,' said Mack, 'I'll lay it on the line. I and the boys are pretty short and we're pretty hungry. You know the price of frogs is twenty for a buck. Now Doc is away and we're hungry. So what we thought is this. We don't want to see you lose nothing, so we'll make over to you twenty-five frogs for a buck. You got a five-frog profit there and nobody loses his shirt.'

'No,' said Lee. 'No money.'

'Well, hell, Lee, all we need is a little groceries. I'll tell you what – we want to give Doc a little party when he gets back. We got plenty of liquor, but we'd like to get maybe some steaks, and stuff like that. He's such a nice guy. Hell, when your wife had that bad tooth, who give her the laudanum?'

Mack had him. Lee was indebted to Doc – deeply indebted. What Lee was having trouble comprehending was how his indebtedness to Doc made it necessary that he give credit to Mack.

'We don't want you to have like a mortgage on frogs,' Mack went on. 'We will actually deliver right into your hands twenty-five frogs for every buck of groceries you let us have and you can come to the party too.'

Lee's mind nosed over the proposition like a mouse in a cheese cupboard. He could find nothing wrong with it. The whole thing was legitimate. Frogs *were* cash as far as Doc was concerned, the price was standard, and Lee had a double profit. He had his five-frog margin and also he had the grocery mark-up. The whole thing hinged on whether they actually had any frogs.

'We go see flog,' Lee said at last.

In front of the Palace he had a drink of the whisky, inspected the damp sack of frogs, and agreed to the transaction. He stipulated, however, that he would take no dead frogs. Now Mack counted fifty frogs into a can and walked back to the grocery with Lee and got two dollars' worth of bacon and eggs and bread.

Lee, anticipating a brisk business, brought a big packing-case out and put it into the vegetable department. He emptied the fifty frogs into it and covered it with a wet gunny-sack to keep his charges happy.

And business was brisk.

Glorious Beer

Beer, the Bible and the seven deadly virtues have made our England what she is.

Oscar Wilde

R H BARHAM *The Ingoldsby Legends*
G FARQUHAR *The Beaux's Stratagem*
E GIBBON *The History of the Decline and Fall of the Roman Empire*
A E HOUSMAN *The Shropshire Lad*

R H Barham

The Reverend Richard Harris Barham: the name has the ring of one of those muscular Victorian clergymen who give their lives to noble but daunting causes such as personally baptizing every single member of India's teeming masses or persuading the natives of a Polynesian archipelago that cricket is more rewarding than cannibalism.

In fact, he was a much more frivolous figure; an author, wit, and congenial drinking companion. His clerical duties at St Paul's allowed plenty of freedom to hold court in a club held in a smoky back room of a nearby tavern with a group of drinking cronies that included Thackeray and, occasionally, Tennyson. The club was called The Deanery, in deference to Barham who was its founder and leading light.

His speciality was humorous verse, and drink features strongly in it; for example:

> Though port should have age
> Yet I don't think it sage
> To entomb it, as some of your connoisseurs do,
> Till it's losing its flavour, and body and hue;
> I question if keeping it does it much good
> After ten years in bottle, and three in the wood.

Another example touches on the method of dealing with the morning after over-indulgence:

> We bore him home and put him to bed
> And we told his wife and daughter
> To give him, next morning, a couple of red
> Herrings, with soda water.

He is best known for *The Ingoldsby Legends*, written under the pseudonym of Thomas Ingoldsby, which were hugely popular in Victorian times, enjoying a kind of cult status. Devotees read these as eagerly as anything by Dickens or Thackeray, knew the farcical plots by heart and were able to identify the real sites on which the fictional places in the *Legends* were based. These were in Kent, where Barham was born in a wealthy middle-class family – his father, an alderman of Canterbury, was a Falstaffian figure of some 19 stones and his clergyman son had a powerful physique.

Among the most popular *Legends* is that of 'The Lay of St Dunstan' which concerns the machinations of a boozy monk in Saxon times who steals St Dunstan's magic broomstick so he can provide himself with an endless supply of ale. The scheme works but is too successful, as the monk cannot stop the flow of ale.

The Ingoldsby Legends

For both now came loaded with Meux's entire;
Combe's, Delafield's, Hanbury's, Truman's – no stopping –
Goding's, Charrington's, Whitbread's continued to drop in
With Hodson's pale ale, from the Sun Brewhouse, Wapping.
(The firms differed then, but I can't put a tax on
My memory to say what their names were in Saxon.)
    To be sure the best beer
    Of all did not appear,
For I've said 'twas June, and so late in the year
The 'Trinity Audit Ale' is not come-at-able,
As I've found to my great grief when dining at that table.

The Lay-Brothers nearest were up to their necks
In an instant, and swimming in strong double X;
While Peter, who spite of himself now had drank hard,
After floating awhile, like a toast in a tankard,
    To the bottom had sunk,
    And was spied by a monk,
Stone-dead, like poor Clarence, half-drown'd and half drunk.

George Farquhar

George Farquhar was one of that marvellous group of Restoration writers whose lives were mirrored in their art, whose subject-matter was their day-to-day existence. They wrote about money and the lack of it, love and the hope of it, and the seemingly endless comedy of society.

The title of Farquhar's first play, *Love and a Bottle*, produced at Drury Lane in 1698, points to at least two of his principal interests. The hero, a self-portrait of the author, was George Roebuck, 'an Irish gentlemen of a wild, roving temper, newly come to London'.

Farquhar was an Irish gentleman, born in Derry, a son of the manse – his father's rectory was burned down by the army of James II – and he is said to have served in the army at the Battle of the Boyne at the age of 13. By the age of 21 he was in London, enjoying the rakish pleasures of the city. He was a classic Restoration figure, a character who might have stepped from the pages of any contemporary play.

Early success as a playwright was followed by money problems, which he attempted to solve by marrying a wealthy heiress, only to discover she was as impoverished as he. A commission in the Grenadiers provided some income, enough money to support his family if not his mistress and his lifestyle.

Army life in the Grenadiers provided the material for *The Recruiting Officer*. He was posted to Shrewsbury, where the play is set, on recruiting duties which involved much time in taverns inducing potential conscripts to enlist, as Sergeant Kite indicates:

> Give me your hand, then; and now, gentlemen, I have no more to say, but this – here's a purse of gold, and there is a tub of humming ale at my quarters! 'Tis the Queen's money, and the Queen's drink – she's a generous queen and loves her subjects – I hope, gentlemen, you won't refuse the Queen's health?

It was performed to great acclaim in 1706, but he returned to the giddy goings-on of society in *The Beaux's Stratagem*, his last play, written in 1707, the year he died at the age of 29.

The Beaux's Stratagem

Scene – An Inn at Lichfield
Enter – Boniface and Aimwell

BONIFACE This way, this way, sir.
AIMWELL You're my landlord, I suppose?

BONIFACE Yes, sir, I'm old Will Boniface; pretty well known upon this road, as the saying is.
AIMWELL Oh, Mr. Boniface, your servant.
BONIFACE Oh, sir, what wilt your honour please to drink, as the saying is?
AIMWELL I have heard your town of Lichfield much famed for ale; I think I'll taste that.
BONIFACE Sir, I have now in my cellar ten tun of the best ale in Staffordshire: 'tis smooth as oil, sweet as milk, clear as amber, and strong as brandy, and will be just fourteen years old the fifth day of next March, old style.
AIMWELL You're very exact, I find, in the age of your ale.
BONIFACE As punctual, sir, as I am in the age of my children. I'll show you such ale. Here, tapster, broach number 1706, as the saying is. Sir, you shall taste my 'anno domini'. I have lived in Lichfield, man and boy, above eight-and-fifty years, and I believe have not consumed eight-and-fifty ounces of meat.
AIMWELL At a meal, you mean, if one may guess by your bulk?
BONIFACE Not in my life, sir; I have fed purely upon ale. I have ate my ale, drank my ale, and I always sleep upon my ale … Now, sir, you shall see … Your worship's health (*Drinks*) Ha! delicious, delicious: fancy it Burgundy, only fancy it – and 'tis worth ten shillings a quart.
AIMWELL (*Drinks*) 'Tis confounded strong.
BONIFACE Strong! It must be so, or how would we be strong that drink it?
AIMWELL And have you lived so long upon this ale, landlord?
BONIFACE Eight-and-fifty years, upon my credit, sir; but it killed my wife, poor woman, as the saying is.
AIMWELL How came that to pass?
BONIFACE I don't know how, sir; she would not let the ale take its natural course, sir; she was for qualifying it every now and then with a dram, as the saying is; and an honest gentleman, that came this way from Ireland, made her a present of a dozen bottles of usquebaugh – but the poor woman was never well after; but, however, I was obliged to the gentleman, you know.
AIMWELL Why, was it the usquebaugh that killed her?
BONIFACE My Lady Bountiful said so. She, good lady, did what could be done; she cured her of three tympanies: but the fourth carried her off; but she's happy, and I'm contented, as the saying is.

AIMWELL Who's that Lady Bountiful you mentioned?
BONIFACE Odds my life, sir, we'll drink her health. (*Drinks*) My Lady Bountiful is one of the best of women. Her last husband, Sir Charles Bountiful, left her worth a thousand pounds a year; and I believe she lays out one-half on't in charitable uses for the good of her neighbours.
AIMWELL Has the lady any children?
BONIFACE Yes, sir, she has a daughter by Sir Charles; the finest woman in all our country, and the greatest fortune. She has a son, too, by her first husband, 'Squire Sullen, who married a fine lady from London t'other day; if you please, sir, we'll drink his health. (*Drinks*)

Edward Gibbon

Although a scholar and historian of distinction, author of *The Decline and Fall of the Roman Empire*, Edward Gibbon suffered the common fate of his age and class: gout.

He confessed the cause to be heavy drinking during a period of service as a young man with the Hampshire militia, on one of his rare absences from the study. The militia's role was more ceremonial than martial but Gibbon found it useful, remarking that the experiences 'of a captain of Hampshire Grenadiers (the reader may smile) has not been useless to the historian of the Roman Empire'. There were disadvantages in his service, though, especially the company of 'our rustic officers who were alike deficient in the knowledge of scholars and the manners of gentlemen'.

However, the commanding officer, Sir Thomas Worsley, was 'an easy, good-humoured man, fond of the table and of his bed … Our conferences were marked by every stroke of the midnight and morning hours, and the same drum which invited him to rest has often summoned me to the parade. His example encouraged the daily practice of hard and even excessive drinking which has sown in my constitution the seeds of the gout.'

Gibbon's descriptions of the country militia echoed comments made a little earlier by John Dryden:

Edward Gibbon

> The country rings around with loud alarms,
> And raw in fields, the rude Militia swarms:
> Mouths without hands maintained at vast expense
> In peace a charge, in war a weak defence.
> Stout once a month they march, a blust'ring band,
> And ever but in times of need at hand.
> This was the morn when, issuing on the guard,
> Drawn up in rank and file they stood prepar'd
> Of seeming arms to make a short essay;
> Then hasten to be drunk, the business of the day.

Before these military adventures the young Gibbon spent nine months in London where he greatly enjoyed the theatre and other attractions. But he warned:

> The pleasures of a town life, the daily round from the tavern to the play, from the play to the coffee house, from the coffee house to the bagnio [a term for upper class brothels] are within the reach of every man who is regardless of his health, his money and his company.

He admitted that 'I was sometimes seduced' but quickly returned to a regime of study and discipline in preparation for his great work which won him fame and a reputation. Not that all were equally impressed. The Duke of Gloucester reacted to the presentation of a copy with: 'Another damned thick, square book. Always scribble, scribble, scribble! Eh, Mr Gibbon?'

Indeed, it was always 'scribble' but to what effect, what gorgeous style. For example, Gibbon observed of the younger Gordian:

> Twentytwo acknowledged concubines and a library of sixtytwo thousand volumes attested the variety of his inclinations: and from the productions he left behind him, it appears that the former as well as the latter were designed for use rather than for ostentation.

A small man, scarcely five feet tall, he grew immensely corpulent, from love of good food and wine. His death at the early age of 53 was rather unexpected, although he had been ill. According to his *valet de chambre*, Gibbon showed a Roman stoicism about the prospect of death, exhibiting 'no sign of alarm or apprehension', and expired after 'consuming a wing of chicken and three glasses of Madeira'.

The History of the Decline and Fall of the Roman Empire

Strong beer, a liquor extracted with very little art from wheat or barley, and *corrupted* (as it is strongly expressed by Tacitus) into a certain semblance of wine, was sufficient for the gross purposes of German debauchery. But those who had tasted the rich wines of Italy, and afterwards of Gaul, sighed for that more delicious species of intoxication. They attempted not, however (as has since been executed with so much success), to naturalize the vine on the banks of the Rhine and the Danube; nor did they endeavour to procure by industry the materials of an advantageous commerce. To solicit by labour what might be ravished by arms was esteemed unworthy of the German spirit. The intemperate thirst of strong liquors often urged the barbarians to invade the provinces on which art or nature had bestowed those much envied presents. The Tuscan who betrayed his country to the Celtic nations attracted them into Italy by the prospect of the rich fruits and delicious wines, the productions of a happier climate. And in the same manner the German auxiliaries, invited into France during the civil wars of the sixteenth century, were allured by the promise of plenteous quarters in the provinces of Champagne and Burgundy. Drunkenness, the most illiberal, but not the most dangerous, of *our* vices, was sometimes capable, in a less civilized state of mankind, of occasioning a battle, a war, or a revolution.

A E Housman

When A E Housman published *The Shropshire Lad* in 1896 his friends and colleagues were astonished that the poem's lusty imbiber of pints and quarts of Ludlow ale could have been created by the distinguished Latin professor of their acquaintance.

The professor of Latin was a classic don: reserved, dry, sceptical, caustic, formidably intelligent. The poem is romantic, sentimental, full of love for the English countryside. But the scholar and the poet had much in common. Housman had a healthy appreciation of beer. A student at University College, London, recalled the aloof figure at lunch where, 'the great man used to surprise us by his immense appetite for beef and beer'.

Fastidious in appearance, austere in manner, Housman loved music halls and ale. He invited a friend to join him on such a trip with the words:

> The form which these orgies take is that after dinner we go to a music hall, and when the music hall closes, as I have no club, we are thrown on the streets and the pothouses: so you know what to expect.

When he left University College for Trinity College, Cambridge, his students presented him with a silver loving cup on which was inscribed some words from his own great poem:

> – malt does more than Milton can
> To justify God's ways to man.

Housman promised he would put the cup to good use at Cambridge, noting: 'Cambridge has seen many strange sights. It has seen Wordsworth drunk; it has seen Porson sober. Now I am a greater scholar than Wordsworth, and a greater poet than Porson, so I fall betwixt and between.'

He regarded beer as restful for the brain, and took it at lunchtime, as the afternoons were the least intellectually demanding part of his day. Stout was a favoured drink for special occasions, especially New Year's Eve, which he always saw in with oysters 'up to 4 doz and drinking all the stout required to wash them down'.

Housman's real love, however, was fine wine, hock and burgundy being his favourites. He was known among his colleagues at the university and his social friends as a discriminating judge of both wine and food.

His publisher, Grant Richards, recalled being entertained at the Café Royal and noted the care with which Housman selected food and wine. 'A Madeira of distinction would begin the meal, and with fish would come … a Johannisberger 74, and then a super Burgundy. Burgundy, white or red, was ever A E H's favourite wine. Port and old brandy followed in their proper places.'

Housman visited France for the first time at the age of 38 and gloried in restaurants such as the Tour d'Argent in Paris where a dish, Barbue Housman, was named after him in recognition of his discernment. Lucky Grant Richards was his guest again:

> With the food a fine white burgundy, followed by a great old burgundy! And coffee … and a fine dating back to the beginning of the last century … that 1907 meal was the finest that he ever gave me.

France yielded more delights for Housman the connoisseur: Chablis Grenouilles 1921 and Nuits Vieilles Vignes 1919 drunk with memorable meals at Chablis; Montrachet 1919 and Meursault Perriers over dinner at Beaune.

Typically, Housman did not over-indulge, remaining as fastidious and austere as ever. His palate, unlike that of most connoisseurs, was unaffacted by age. When in a rest home and aged more than 70 he enjoyed lunches of oysters and champagne. Oysters and stout remained a year-end treat and he continued to savour his beloved burgundy until his final year.

The Shropshire Lad

Terence, this is stupid stuff

Terence, this is stupid stuff:
You eat your victuals fast enough;
There can't be much amiss, 'tis clear,
To see the rate you drink your beer.
But oh, good Lord, the verse you make,
It gives a chap the belly-ache.
The cow, the old cow, she is dead;
It sleeps well, the horned head:
We poor lads, 'tis our turn now
To hear such tunes as killed the cow.
Pretty friendship 'tis to rhyme

Your friends to death before their time
Moping melancholy mad:
Come, pipe a tune to dance to, lad.

Why, if 'tis dancing you would be,
There's brisker pipes than poetry.
Say, for what were hop-yards meant,
Or why was Burton built on Trent?
Oh many of peer of England brews
Livelier liquor than the Muse,
And malt does more than Milton can
To justify God's ways to man.
Ale, man, ale's the stuff to drink
For fellows whom it hurts to think:
Look into the pewter pot
To see the world as the world's not.
And faith, 'tis pleasant till 'tis past:
The mischief is that 'twill not last.

Oh I have been to Ludlow fair
And left my necktie God knows where,
And carried half-way home, or near,
Pints and quarts of Ludlow beer:
Then the world seemed none so bad,
And I myself a sterling lad;
And down in lovely muck I've laid,
Happy till I woke again.
Then I saw the morning sky:
Heigho, the tale was all a lie;
The world, it was the old world yet,
I was I, my things were wet,
And nothing now remained to do
But begin the game anew.

Therefore, since the world has still,
Much good, but much less good than ill,
And the sun and moon endure
Luck's a chance, but trouble's sure,
I'd face it as a wise man would,
And train for ill and not for good.
'Tis true, the stuff I bring for sale

Is not so brisk a brew as ale:
Out of a stem that scored the hand
I wrung it in a weary land,
But take it: if the smack is sour,
The better for the embittered hour;
It should do good to heart and head
When your soul is in my soul's stead;
And I will friend you, if I may,
In the dark and cloudy day.

There was a king reigned in the East;
There, when kings will sit to feast,
They get their fill before they think
With poisoned meat and poisoned drink.
He gathered all that springs to birth
From the many-venomed earth;
First a little, thence to more,
He sampled all her killing store;
And easy, smiling, seasoned sound,
Sate the king when healths went round.
They put arsenic in his meat
And stared aghast to watch him eat;
They poured strychnine in his cup
And shook to see him drink it up:
They shook, they stared as white's their shirt:
Them it was their poison hurt.
– I tell the tale that I heard told,
Mithridates, he died old.

In Praise of Wine

Good wine kept here, against your coming.

François Rabelais

H BALZAC	*The Red House*
COLETTE	*Earthly Paradise*
N DOUGLAS	*Old Calabria*
E FITZGERALD	*Rubaiyat of Omar Khayyam*
J W GOETHE	*Faust*
HORACE	*First Book of Epistles*
J KEATS	'Hence Burgundy, Claret, and Port', 'Ode to a Nightingale', 'Lamia'
L LEE	*Cider with Rosie*
G MEREDITH	*The Egoist*
W SCOTT	*Peveril of the Peak*
A TROLLOPE	*The Prime Minister*

Honoré de Balzac

Balzac was a life force, a volcano of a man with apparently inexhaustible supplies of energy and enthusiasm, a man beside whom even such a ferociously driven writer as Dickens seems an idle dilettante.

Honoré de Balzac was prodigal in all things. Some 143 titles were planned for *La Comédie humaine* and 80 were completed by his death. Apart from these major novels, he poured out a flood of plays, essays and short stories. He made and lost fortunes, loved widely and recklessly and was often described as a madman and a genius, sometimes in the same breath.

Balzac was a gourmet, one who regarded his stomach with something like veneration; but he had odd tastes, devouring dozens of pears at a sitting. He stored them with care – at one time the total stood at 1,500. It is unlikely that the eighteenth-century gourmet, Brillat-Savarin, whom Balzac admired, would have approved of this excess. Another contemporary observer remarked that Balzac was the favourite author of gluttons.

He was not a heavy drinker. Indeed, he was usually extraordinarily abstemious, drinking water and endless cups of scaldingly hot coffee through the night while he worked in his study. When he did drink, however, he was typically wholehearted and could consume prodigious amounts without becoming even slightly drunk.

'I am an expensive guest,' he said. Vouvray was a favoured drink, unsurprisingly for a son of the Loire, and he also enjoyed champagne. Coming from a wine region, he had a wide knowledge of viniculture, which is reflected in many of his books. Graham Robb, in his fine study of Balzac, says that *La Comédie humaine* is crammed with details of dishes and drinks – wines from thirteen different regions of France and nine from abroad.

The Red House

'Oh! as to victuals,' said the landlord, jerking his head, 'people come to the Red House for ten leagues round for wedding feasts.

You shall have a banquet fit for a prince, fish from the Rhine! That tells you everything.'

When they had given over their tired beasts into the host's care, they left him to shout in vain for the stable folk, and went into the public room of the inn. It was so full of dense white clouds blown from the pipes of a room-full of smokers, that at first they could not make out what kind of company they had fallen among; but after they had sat for a while at a table, and put in practice the patience of travelled philosophers who know when it is useless to make a fuss, they gradually made out the inevitable accessories of a German inn. The stove, the clock, the tables, pots of beer and long pipes, loomed out through the tobacco smoke; so did the faces of the motley crew, Jews, Germans, and whatnot, with one or two rough boatmen thrown in.

The epaulettes of a few French officers shone through the thick mist, and spurs and sabres clanked incessantly upon the flag-stones. Some were playing at cards, the rest quarrelling among themselves, or were silent, ate, or drank, and came or went ...

Gradually the noise diminished, the travellers went off one by one, the clouds of tobacco smoke cleared away. By the time that the table was set for the assistant surgeons, and the classic carp of the Rhine appeared, it was eleven o'clock and the room was empty. Through the stillness of the night it was possible to hear faint noises of horses stamping or crunching their provender, the ripple of the Rhine, the vague indefinable sounds in an inn full of people when everyone has retired to rest.

Colette

Colette was the most sensual of writers. No one has captured place and time – the earth, sky, smells, light, heat – more vividly, more precisely than she.

She was also a deeply sensuous human being with a deep love, a passion, for food and, above all, wine. She was fortunate in a number of ways, born in Burgundy into a family where the values of wine were well understood. As she said herself, 'Since childhood I have known French wine, and been well acquainted with it.'

Colette

Someone said of her once: 'She likes everything she likes rather too much, as children do.' She, however, thought of herself as restrained, a little austere and certainly not indulgent. And she was right, by her own standards, despite the fact that she was a rotund 13 stone in the 1930s as a consequence of her love for food and wine.

She was a proud peasant in her tastes. Maurice, her third husband, described her as 'French to her fingertips and, above all, provincial ... She was provincial in the art of living, the economical recipes, the tidy cupboards, the provisions, she was provincial in her punctuality, her proverbs, in boxwood and lily-of-the-valley, in *galette des rois*, mulled wine, log fires, chestnuts, and slow cooking under the ashes.'

Her favourite supper was typically peasant-like – a big wedge of cheese, a knob of bread from a round loaf and a glass of wine. And she had a peasant's triumph in a bargain, remembering with pleasure, years later, a trip to Franche Comte where she had picked up fine wines for a few francs from a wayside inn that was changing hands – Volnay, Chambertin, Corton and a 40-year-old Frontignan, 'glowing with amber and warmth'.

Her reaction to places was often brisk and uncomplicated, as in the case of Bordeaux which she described as a 'fine town, full of grub and tipple'.

Admirers claim – and it is difficult to argue with them – that reading her prose on the pleasures of food and wine is as intoxicating as drinking itself.

Colette's idyllic days at her house at St Tropez, *La Treille Muscate*, 'in the climate of another world', are remembered: the small, low-ceilinged house in 'four acres, a vine, orange trees, fig trees with green fruit, fig trees with black fruit' and the furrows between the vines, 'brimming with garlic, with pimentos, with aubergines'. It was here that meals were taken on the terrace, in the shade of a trellis of wisteria and vines, fish from the nearby sea, vegetables from the garden and cooling wine from the property's vines which yielded a rich harvest of some 1,500 bottles a year. These were the young wines she loved as well as the finest wines in her cellar, cool wines that flowed easily from the throat and hardly troubled the kidneys, wines that could be drunk by the pint in the hot days of a southern summer.

Earthly Paradise

I was very well brought up. As a first proof of so categorical a statement, I shall simply say that I was no more than three years old when my father poured out my first full liqueur glass of an amber-coloured wine which was sent up to him from the Midi, where he was born: the muscat of Frontignan.

The sun breaking from behind clouds, a shock of sensuous pleasure, an illumination of my newborn tastebuds! This initiation ceremony rendered me worthy of wine for all time. A little later I learned to empty my goblet of mulled wine, scented with cinnamon and lemon, as I ate a dinner of boiled chestnuts. At an age when I could still scarcely read, I was spelling out, drop by drop, old light clarets and dazzling Yquems. Champagne appeared in its turn, a murmur of foam, leaping pearls of air providing an accompaniment to birthday and First Communion banquets, complementing the grey truffles from La Puisaye … Good lessons, from which I graduated to a familiar and discreet use of wine, not gulped down greedily but measured out into narrow glasses, assimilated mouthful by spaced-out, meditative mouthful.

It was between my eleventh and fifteenth years that this admirable education programme was perfected. My mother was afraid that I was outgrowing my strength and was in danger of a 'decline'. One by one, she unearthed, from their bed of dry sand, certain bottles that had been ageing beneath our house in a cellar – which is, thanks be to God, still intact – hewn out of fine, solid granite. I feel envious, when I think back, of the privileged little urchin I was in those days. As an accompaniment to my modest, fill-in meals – a chop, a leg of cold chicken, or one of those hard cheeses, 'baked' in the embers of a wood fire and so brittle that one blow of the fist would shatter them into pieces like a pane of glass – drank Chateau-Laffittes, Chambertins, and Cortons which had escaped capture by the 'Prussians' in 1870. Certain of these wines were already fading, pale and scented still like a dead rose; they lay on a sediment of tannin that darkened their bottles, but most of them retained their aristocratic ardour and their invigorating powers. The good old days!

… The vine and the wine it produces are two great mysteries. Alone in the vegetable kingdom, the vine makes the true savour of the earth intelligible to man. With what fidelity it makes the translation! It senses, then expresses, in its clusters of fruit the secrets of the soil. The flint, through the vine, tells us that it is living, fusible, a giver of nourishment. Only in wine does the ungrateful chalk pour out its golden tears. A vine, transported across mountains and over seas, will struggle to keep its personability, and sometimes triumphs over the powerful chemistries of the mineral world. Harvested near Algiers, a white wine will still remember without fail, year after year, the noble Bordeaux graft that gave it exactly the right hint of sweetness, lightened its body, and endowed it with gaiety. And it is far-off Jerez that gives its warmth and colour to the dry and cordial wine that ripens at Chateau Chalon, on the summit of a narrow, rocky plateau ...

The present snobbery about food is producing a crop of hostelries and country inns the like of which has never been seen before. Wine is revered in these places. Can wisdom be born again from a faith so unenlightened, a faith professed by mouths already, alas, armoured with cocktails, with venomous aperitifs, with harsh and numbing spirits? Let us hope that it can. As old age approaches, I offer, as my contribution, the example of a stomach without remorse or damage, a very well-disposed liver, and a still sensitive palate, all preserved by good and honest wine. Therefore, wine, fill up this glass I now hold out to you! A delicate and simple glass, a light bubble in which there play the sanguine fires of a great Burgundian ancestor, the topaz of Yquem, and the balas ruby, sometimes with a paler purple tinge, of the Bordeaux with its scent of violets ...

There comes a time of life when one begins to prize young wine. On a Southern shore there is a string of round, wicker-covered demijohns always kept in store for me. One grape harvest fills them to the brim, then the next grape harvest finding them empty once more, in its turn fills them up again. Perhaps you have a hoard of fine old wines in your cellar, but do not disdain these wines because they give such quick returns; they are clear, dry, various, they flow easily from the throat down to the kidneys and scarcely pause a moment there. Even when it is of a warmer constitution, down there, if the day is a really hot one, we think nothing of drinking down a good pint of this particular wine, for it refreshes you and leaves a double taste behind, of muscat and of cedarwood.

Norman Douglas

Norman Douglas is best known today as the author of that dazzling novel, *South Wind*, but among his friends his distinction as a writer was almost equalled by his reputation as a connoisseur of the unusual in food and wine. His tastes were decidedly original. His publisher recalled a 'startling' dinner in Florence in 1930:

> Grey truffles cooked with cheese in sizzling pannikins, the stench dreadful but the taste good, a licentious dish. Then a remarkable stew of jugged hare with an oriental-like sauce compounded of currants, pine-nuts and chocolate, corrected with vinegar, a dish fit for the Caliph. And a paunch of white Chianti, rare and very special, that swung amorously in its shining cradle.

Douglas was intensely sociable and loved arranging feasts of this kind for his friends. Like Dr Johnson, he preferred dining in public rather than at home, favouring small, peasant-like restaurants where he would search for unusual dishes and country wines, although he was often highly critical of the wines that came his way, labelling them 'muck'.

In general, he drank the wine of the area in which he was living. In Florence, it was Chianti; in Calabria it was Ciro, whenever it could be found. The latter is reputed to be the oldest wine in the world, a descendant of the wines served to victorious athletes in the original Olympic Games in Greece.

He was certainly no wine snob. Richard Aldington complained bitterly of his lack of taste in wine on at least two occasions – of drinking *vin ordinaire* in a grand restaurant in Cannes and of not appreciating the best local wines Aldington had collected when Douglas stayed with him in the South of France. Aldington seems to have been easily offended by Douglas in these matters – he even complained when Douglas bought a couple of bottles of vintage champagne and ham sandwiches in a local café, seeing it as a slight on his hospitality.

What is certain is that Douglas drank a lot of whatever was available, which was usually flask after flask of Chianti. He was fond of champagne, once suggesting that if somebody would stand him half a bottle of champagne around eleven in the morning it would help him write – a sound idea, it seems to me, especially if it is vintage champagne.

Most of Douglas's life was spent in Italy, primarily in Florence, Capri and Calabria, places described in classics such as *Siren Land* and *Old Calabria*. His literary friends in the 1920s included D H Lawrence and Middleton Murray, as well as Aldington, and many then successful writers whose books have long since vanished from most bookshelves. Later friends and admirers included Graham Greene and Elizabeth David, the cookery writer, who quoted in *Italian Food* his amusing and learned observations on Italian fish soup, *zuppa di pesce*, for which 'Neapolitans sell their female relatives' but which he could not bear, although he conceded that 'copious libations' would do wonders for it.

Old Calabria

One might say much in praise of Calabrian wine. The land is full of pleasant surprises for the oenophilist, and one of these days I hope to embody my experiences in the publication of a wine chart of the province with descriptive text running alongside – the purchasers of which, if few, will certainly be of the right kind.

The wine of Ciro, for instance, is purest nectar and so is that which grows still nearer at hand in the classical vale of Neto and was praised, long ago, by old Pliny; and so are at least two dozen more. For even as Gregorvorious says that the smallest Italian community possesses its duly informed antiquarian, if you can but put your hand upon him, so, I may be allowed to add, every little place hereabouts can boast of at least one individual who will give you good wine, provided – provided you go properly to work to find him.

Now although, when young, the Calabrian Bacchus has a wild *beatue du diable* which appeals to one's expansive moods, he already begins to totter, at seven years of age, in sour decrepitude. To pounce upon him at the psychological moment, to discover in whose cool and cobwebby cellar he is dreaming out his golden summer of manhood – that is what a foreigner can never, never hope to achieve, without competent local aid.

To this end, I generally apply to the priests; not because they are the greatest drunkards (far from it; they are mildly epicurean or even abstemious) but by reason of their unrivalled knowledge of personalities. They know exactly who has been able to keep his liquor of such and such a year, and who has been obliged to sell or partially adulterate it; they know, from the confessional of the wives, the why and wherefore of all such private family affairs and share, with the chemist, the gift of seeing furthest into the tangled web of home life. They are ‘gi[illegible]si’ however, of these acquirements and must be approached in the right spirit – a spirit of humility. But if you tactfully lead up to the subject by telling him of the manifold hardships of travel in foreign lands, the discomfort of life in hostelries, the food that leaves so much to be desired and, above all, the coarse wine that is already beginning, you greatly fear, to injure your sensitive spleen (an important organ in Calabria) inducing a hypochondriacal tendency to see all the beauties of this fair land in an odious and sombre light – turning your day into night as it were – it must be an odd priest, indeed, who is not compassionately moved to impart the desired information regarding the whereabouts of the best *vino di famiglia* at that moment obtainable.

And failing the priests, I go to an elderly individual of that tribe of red-nosed connoisseurs, the coachmen, ever thirsty and mercenary souls.

Edward Fitzgerald

Even if Edward Fitzgerald had been the most rigid of abstainers, which he was not, he would deserve a place in this book as the translator of the *Rubaiyat of Omar Khayyam*, the most popular bibulous work in the language. The work itself is more than a poem; it is an expression of a philosophy that has appealed to generations of drinking men, has been memorized and quoted, often at inordinate length, wherever drinkers gather and glasses are raised.

> Drink! for you know not whence you came, nor why:
> Drink! for you know not why you go, nor where.

Lines such as these, and there are many of them, appear to gain even greater significance as the second and third bottles come and go.

Fitzgerald, the man responsible for bringing the reflections of an eleventh-century Persian poet to the attention of nineteenth-century readers, was not some intrepid explorer who had read the lines on the wall of an ancient temple. He was a rich, reclusive eccentric and scholar who preferred to spend most of his life in the depths of East Anglia.

Fitzgerald was less odd and less reclusive when young. At Cambridge he made lifelong friendships with a number of young men who became the leading literary figures of the day, Tennyson and Thackeray among them.

His drinking habits were neither excessive nor unusual but his approach to food was decidedly eccentric. 'Boiled leg of pork, parmesan cheese, and a glass of port, maketh a dinner for a prince' is a recommended meal. Further evidence of his individual hospitality came from a Norfolk friend, Bernard Barton:

> Tom Churchyard drove me over last night to a Symposium given by Edw Fitzgerald to us two, and old Crabbe – lots of palaver, smoking and laughing – my head swims yet with the fumes, and odours of the baccy and my sides are sore with laughing ... It was the oddest melange! Tea, Porter, Ale, Wine, Brandy, Cigars – Cold Lamb, Cucumber – Bread & Cheese – no precise line of demarcation between tea – and Supper – it was one continuous spread something coming on fresh every ten minutes – till we wonder'd where they came, and where they could be put.

As a wealthy man, Fitzgerald had no need to work, but he interested himself in literature, especially the classics, in the manner of a cultivated man of leisure. Remarkably, at the age of 43 he began to study Persian and had translated and published at his own expense the quatrains or *rubaiyat* of Omar by the time he was 50. The work attracted no interest and seemed destined to be lost for ever, perhaps a predictable fate for what had been an agreeable diversion for a wealthy, scholarly man to while away his time. Two hundred and fifty copies were printed but so few were sold that the bookseller put the remainder in a bargain box outside his shop at a price of 1*d*. A copy came into the hands of Dante Gabriel Rossetti and from him reached other members of the Pre-Raphaelite Brotherhood, at last coming to the august mentor of the movement, John Ruskin. It became famous in Britain and America, has been published in hundreds of editions, is a constant in all the anthologies, and continues as a source of refreshment for drinkers.

Rubaiyat of Omar Khayyam

Awake! For Morning in the Bowl of Night
Has flung the Stone that puts the Stars to Flight:
And Lo! the Hunter of the East has caught
The Sultan's Turret in a Noose of Light.

Wake! For the sun who scatter'd into flight
The Stars before him from the Field of Night,
Drives Night along with them from Heav'n, and strikes
The Sultan's Turret with a Shaft of Light.

Dreaming when Dawn's Left Hand was in the Sky
I heard a Voice within the Tavern cry,
'Awake, my Little ones, and fill the Cup
Before Life's Liquor in its Cup be dry'.

Before the phantom of False morning died,
Methought a Voice within the Tavern cried,
'When all the Temple is prepared within,
Why nods the drowsy Worshipper outside?'

Iram indeed is gone with all its Rose,
And Jamshyd's Se'n-ring'd Cup where no one knows;
But still the Vine her ancient Ruby yields,
And still a Garden by the Water blows.

Come, fill the Cup, and in the fire of Spring
Your Winter Garment of Repentance fling:
The Bird of Time has but a little way
To flutter – and the Bird is on the wing.

Here with Loaf of Bread beneath the bough,
A flask of Wine, a Book of Verse – and Thou
Beside me singing in the Wilderness –
And Wilderness were Paradise enow!

Lo! some we loved, the loveliest and best
That Time and Fate of all their Vintage prest,
Have drunk their Cup a Round or two before,
And one by one crept silently to Rest.

Ah, make the most of what we yet may spend,
Before we too into the Dust descend;
  Dust into Dust, and under Dust, to lie,
Sans Wine, sans Song, sans Singer, and sans End!

What, without asking, hither hurried *whence*?
And, without asking, *whether* hurried hence!
  Another and another Cup to drown
The Memory of this Impertinence!

Ah, fill the Cup: – what boots it to repeat
How Time is slipping underneath our Feet:
  Unborn TOMORROW, and dead YESTERDAY,
Why fret about them if TODAY be sweet!

And much as Wine has play'd the Infidel,
And robb'd me of my Robe of Honour – Well
  I wonder often what the Vintners buy
One half so precious as the Goods they sell.

Johann Wolfgang von Goethe

Goethe has something of the reputation of an awesome peak in a mountain range: splendid viewed from afar but too glacial and forbidding to be approached closely. Given his formidable reputation as a poet, philosopher, playwright, novelist, artist and administrator it is somehow reassuring to find he had human frailties and failings. It is not my intention to suggest Goethe was a hero with feet of clay; hollow legs, more likely, because he was an enthusiastic and confirmed toper for most of his long life.

One of his early plays, he admitted, was written on a Sunday afternoon, with the help of a bottle of burgundy. In the one work with which most of us are at all familiar, *Faust*, Mephistopheles speaks of the mysteries of wine-making and of Frankfurt's famous and deadly cider, Eppelwoi. This work is studded with references to drink, often to beer. A student declares:

Stiff beer, biting tobacco and a girl
In her smart dress are the best things I know.

Goethe's fondness for wine no doubt began in childhood. At the family home in Frankfurt the cellars held a massive stock of fine wines in barrel, some from the classic vintage of 1706. When the cellar flooded Goethe remembered hopping from barrel to barrel. The smell of the wine permeated the house, an ineradicable memory of childhood.

Naturally, as a good German and one living in an area with a proud tradition of the art of brewing, he had a discriminating taste for fine beer. As a student in Leipzig he learned to appreciate the delights of Munich beer, and much later, when in Rome, he talked and drank well into the night with expatriate friends, drinking locally brewed German beer.

While dining in an inn, drinking wine diluted with water, Goethe was mocked by a gang of rowdy students at the next table. He responded immediately with the following little poem:

Wasser allein macht stumm,
das beweisen im Teiche die Fische,
Wein allein macht dumm,
das beweisen die Herren am Tische.
Weil ich weder das eine noch das anders will sein,
drum drink ich mit Wasser vermischt den Wein.

Drinking only water makes you dumb
like the fish in the pond.
Drinking wine alone makes you foolish
like the gentlemen at that table.
As I don't wish to be like either of them
I drink my wine mixed with water.

When Goethe was ill and unable to eat, friends fed him the local dark beer, Kostritzer Schwarzbier, a beer like stout and thought to have had medicinal qualities. It is not possible to validate these claims but he recovered.

Goethe's fame in his lifetime was widespread and became even greater in the years following his death. He was venerated as a sage, regarded as a superhuman figure, like a Shakespeare or a Plato, on an altogether more elevated plane than the rest of humanity. But he was also a man who enjoyed a bottle or three, at home or on his travels – sipping the local Lacryma Christi while surveying the ruins of Pompeii, for example.

Age did not cramp his style, as the young Thackeray reported when he met the master in Weimar (a visit Thackeray described as like going to the dentist) when Goethe was in his eighties, still working and still calling for more wine.

Faust

To the Glass

Old friends were gathered all,
And thou with mirth didst light grave features up,
On days of high festivity,
And family solemnity,
As each to each passed on the happy cup;
Its massy pride, the figures rich and old,
Of curious carving, and the merry task
Of each (thus did our pleasant customs ask)
Who drank, the quaint old symbols to unfold,
In rhymes made at the moment; then the mask
Of serious seeming, as at one long draught
Each guest the full deep goblet duly quaffed;
The old cup, the old customs, the old rhymes,
All now are with me: all, that of old times
Can speak, are speaking to my heart; the nights
Of boyhood, and their manifold delights;
Oh never more to gay friend sitting next
Shall my hand reach thee; never more from me
Shall merry rhyme illustrate the old text,
And into meaning read each mystery;
This is the draught that, if the brain still think,
Will set it thinking in another mood;
Old cup, now fill thee with the dark brown flood;
It is my choice; I mixed it, and will drink:
My last draught this on earth I dedicate,
(And with it be my heart and spirit borne!)
A festal offering to the rising morn …
    Bower on bower,
    Tendril and flower;
    Clustering grapes,
    This vine's purple treasure,
    Have fallen in the wine-vat,

And bleed in its pressure
Foaming and steaming, the new wine is streaming,
Over agate and amethyst,
Rolls from its fountain,
Leaving behind it
Meadow and mountain,
And the hill-slopes smile greener, far down where it breaks
Into billowy streamlets, or lingers in lakes.
And the winged throng, drinking deep of delight
From the rivers of joy, are pursuing their flight …

Horace

The character of the Roman poet, Horace, as it appears in his work, is eminently sane and civilized. He observed life with a clear eye and recorded the foibles of men and women with wry wit. He was not a poet in the romantic mould, heaving with hopeless passions, and not one who would die for love. Indeed, it seems likely that Horace had a keener passion for wine, which is a constant theme in his poems, as it was a constant in Roman life.

In a poem to Postumus he warns of the folly of hoarding fine wine which will only be gulped by a lucky heir:

A worthier heir thy Caecuban will waste,
Locked with a hundred keys; and, stained with wine
Inestimable, thy paved floor will shine,
Wine which a pontiff's banquet should have graced.

There is also practical advice on handling wine:

If under a cloudless sky
You set Massic wine, whatever coarseness is in it
The night air will refine and the smell pass off
Which gets on the nerve so; but should you strain it through linen,
The wine is spoiled by losing its full-bodied flavour.

A man who has learned the trick will mix the wine
That comes from Surrentum with dregs of Falernian wine,
Collecting the sediment there with a pigeon's egg,
For the yolk sinks to the bottom, tumbling with it
All foreign matter.

The much-praised Falernian is also recommended in cooking:

Supposing a friend
Drops in of an evening, say, without any warning,
And you fear a tough old hen won't be to his taste,
Be clever and plunge it in diluted Falernian;
That will render it tender.

He writes of a luxurious dinner party with the choicest wines:

Caecuban wine,
And Alcon with Chian without any sea-water in it.
'If Alban attracts you more than the wines just served,
Maecenas,' our host said, 'or else Falernian, tell me;
We have them both.'

Horace clearly had a cultivated man's knowledge of wine and evidently enjoyed it:

What magic is there a good, long drink cannot work?
It brings what's hidden to light, tells hope to stand firm,
Prods cowardly men into battle, raises the load
From hearts burdened with trouble, teaches new arts.
Who is the man that a bowl brimming with wine
Has failed to make eloquent?

It was a subject close to his heart, as is seen in his ode to a bottle:

O goodly bottle, of an age with me;
When Manlius was consul we were born;
Whether strife, mirth or quarrels are in thee,
Or raging love, or easy sleep till morn.

First Book of Epistles

To Maecenas

If what you take as true old Cratinus asserted,
Learned Maecenas, no poems can give any pleasure,
None live very long, that are written by drinkers of water.
Ever since Bacchus enlisted the raving poets
Among the Satyrs and Fauns, as a general rule
The sweet Muses have smelt of wine in the morning.
His praises of wine convince us that Homer drank;
Father Ennius himself never darted forth to describe
Battle-scenes, unless he'd been heavily drinking.
'To the sober, to those who keep dry, I give in charge
The Forum and Libo's Well-head, the world of business;
Those who abstain from wine I shall bar from singing.'
From the very moment I issued this edict of mine,
The poets have never stopped having their nightly contests
In drinking wine, and reeking of drink all day.

John Keats

Keats is the perfect image of the classic poet: young, rapturous, gifted and doomed. He could have been a creation of some other writer's pen, the tragic hero of an opera or Gothic novel. The image is true enough but he was also a young man who enjoyed good company, good wine, and bawdy jokes. Claret was a favourite drink – he had a habit of covering his tongue with cayenne pepper which was intended to make him better able to savour the wine.

He sang the praises of claret in a letter to his brother, George, in February 1819:

> I like claret … For really 'tis so fine – it fills one's mouth with a gushing freshness – then goes down cool and feverless – then you do not feel it quarrelling with your liver – no, it is rather a Peacemaker, and lies as quietly as it did in the grape; then it is as fragrant as the Queen Bee. And the more ethereal part of it mounts

> into the Brain, not assaulting the cerebral apartments like a bully in a badhouse looking for his trull, and hurrying from door to door bouncing against the wainscot, but rather walks like Aladdin about his enchanted palace so gently that you do not feel his step.

He loved parties, staying up all night, drinking, playing cards. It should be remembered he was a young man on the town – he was only 25 when he died – following the pursuits and pastimes available to a young man in London. He enjoyed drinking with actors in Drury Lane, admiring their couldn't-give-a-damn manners.

Snatches of verse often appear in his letters, such as:

Give me women, wine and snuff
Until I cry out: 'Hold, enough!'
You may do so sans objection
Till the day of resurrection;
For bless my beard they aye shall be
My beloved Trinity.

The lines may not be immortal but they convey the spirit of a young man on the spree. His high spirits were shared by his friends. An 'immortal' dinner organized by his friend, the painter Benjamin Haydon, turned into a boisterous evening. Other guests included Wordsworth – who did not allow the levity of others to interfere with his solemn declamations of verse – Charles Lamb, who got very tight, and Keats who had the giggles at Lamb's antics.

Haydon remembered another jolly evening when he, Keats and another friend spend the whole time imitating the sounds of musical instruments 'till we were ready to burst with laughing'.

Before Keats became ill, he enjoyed several walking tours, one as far as what he called 'John 'o Grots', where it rained heavily and he drank whiskey. In Ireland there was more rain and more whiskey (at that time the spelling used by Keats was common in both countries).

Hence Burgundy, Claret, and Port

Hence Burgundy, Claret, and Port,
   Away with old Hock and Madeira,
Two couthly ye are for my sport;

There's a beverage brighter and clearer.
Instead of a pitiful rummer,
My wine overbrims a whole summer;
My bowl is the sky,
And I drink at my eye,
Till I feel in the brain
A Delphian pain –
Then follow, my Caius! then follow!
On the green of the hill
We will drink our fill
Of golden sunshine,
Till our brains intertwine
With the glory and grace of Apollo!

Ode to a Nightingale

II

Oh, for a draught of vintage! that hath been
Cooled a long age in the deep-delvèd earth,
Tasting of Flora and the country green,
Dance, and Provençal song, and sunburnt mirth!
Oh, for a beaker full of the warm South,
Full of the true, the blushful Hippocrene,
With beaded bubbles winking at the brim,
And purple-stained mouth,
That I might drink, and leave the world unseen,
And with thee fade away into the forest dim—

Lamia

While fluent Greek a vowelled undersong
Kept up among the guests, discoursing low
At first, for scarcely was the wine at flow;
But when the happy vintage touched their brains,
Louder they talk, and louder come the strains
Of powerful instruments. The gorgeous dyes,

The space, the splendour of the draperies,
The roof of awful richness, nectareous cheer,
Beautiful slaves, and Lamia's self, appear,
Now, when the wine has done its rosy deed
And every soul from human trammels freed,
No more so strange; for merry wine, sweet wine,
Will make Elysian shades not too fair, too divine.
Soon was God Bacchus at meridian height;
Flushed were their cheeks, and bright eyes double bright;
Garlands of every green, and every scent
From vales deflowered, or forest-trees branch-rent,
In baskets of bright osiered gold were brought
High as the handles heaped, to suit the thought
Of every guest – that each, as he did please,
Might fancy-fit his brows, silk-pillowed at his ease.

Laurie Lee

A minor theme of Laurie Lee's autobiographical trilogy is his progress and education in the art of drinking. In the famous first part, *Cider with Rosie*, there is childish lemonade and ginger beer, beer-drinking uncles, and, of course, memorably, cider:

> Never to be forgotten, that first long secret drink of golden fire, juice of those valleys and of that time, wine of wild orchards, of russett summer, of plump red apples.

Drinking looms large in *As I Walked Out One Midsummer Morning*, that haunting description of a solitary exploration on foot in the vastness of Spain in the 1930s. 'Warmed to idiocy by wine', he played his fiddle to peasants in remote villages, wandered from bar to bar in Valladolid, drinking glasses of 'clotted wine'. There were goblets of golden sherry in Madrid, glasses of fiery cognac everywhere, raw wine of Shulomonon at less than a penny a glass. The young man, only 19, was struck by the ease with which the Spaniards drank, naturally accepting 'one of the natural privileges of living'.

In Toledo he met the poet Roy Campbell who claimed to drink four and a half litres of the local wine each day 'thin, sharp stuff, lobster pink in colour and one of the consolations of living in Toledo'. After the tidal flow of wine at lunchtime they drank brandy in the evenings, smooth and warm and straight from the cask.

In bad weather, holed up on the coast of Andalucia, he joined the locals in the bars for long sessions drinking crude brandy mixed with boiling water while the rain drummed at the windows. Despite the long hours, there was no drunkenness, he remembered, although he would sometimes experience 'moments of that pure, almost virginal intoxication, to which all subsequent drinking tries in vain to return'.

There are no lyrical descriptions of drinking in the final part of the trilogy, *A Moment of War*. It is a bleak time of privation, ugliness and war – of thin wine, a time when drink was a means of escape, of oblivion.

Laurie Lee eventually left foreign parts, coming full circle in old age to his home village in Gloucestershire, the starting point of his adventures; back to his roots, to the local pub, to drinks of whisky and beer (but never, as he revealed to a magazine in 1995, cider).

Cider with Rosie

Granny Wallon's wines were famous in the village and she spent a large part of her year preparing them. The gathering of the ingredients was the first of the mysteries. At the beginning of April she would go off with her baskets and work round the fields and hedges, and every fine day till the end of summer would find her somewhere out in the valley. One saw her come hobbling home in the evening, bearing her cargoes of crusted flowers, till she had buckets of cowslips, dandelions, elder-blossom crammed into every corner of the house. The elder-flowers, drying on her kitchen floor, seemed to cover it with a rancid carpet, a crumbling rime of grey-green blossom fading fast in a dust of summer. Later the tiny grape-cluster of the elderberry itself would be seething in purple vats, with daisies and orchids thrown in to join it, even strands of the dog-rose bush.

What seasons fermented in Granny Wallon's kitchen, what summers were brought to the boil, with limp flower-heads piled around the floor holding fast to their clotted juices – the sharp spiced honey of those cowslips first, then the coppery reeking dandelion, the bitter poppy's whiff of powder, the cat's breath, death-green elder. Gleanings of days and a dozen pastures, strippings of lanes and hedges – she bore them home to her flag-tiled kitchen, sorted them each from each, built up her fires and loaded her pots, and added her sugar and yeast. The vats boiled daily in suds and sugar, steamy, embalmed, distilled the hot dews and flowery soups and ran the wine down the dripping walls.

And not only flower-heads went into these brews; the old lady used parsnips, too, potatoes, sloes, crab-apples, quinces, in fact anything she could lay her hands on. Granny Wallon made wine as though demented, out of anything at all; and no doubt, if given enough sugar and yeast, could have made a drink out of a box of old matches.

She never hurried or hoarded her wines, but led them gently through their natural stages. After the boiling they were allowed to settle and to work in the cool of the vats. For several months, using pieces of toast, she scooped off their yeasty sediments. Then she bottled and labelled each liquor in turn and put them away for a year.

At last one was ready, then came the day of distribution. A squeak and a rattle would shake our window, and we'd see the old lady, wispily grinning, waving a large white jug in her hand. 'Hey there, missus! Try this'n, then. It's the first of my last year's cowslip.'

Through the kitchen window she'd fill up our cups and watch us, head cocked, while we drank. The wine in the cups was still and golden, transparent as a pale spring morning. It smelt of ripe grass in some far-away field and its taste was as delicate as air. It seemed so innocent, we would swig away happily and even the youngest guzzled it down. Then a curious rocking would seize the head; tides rose from our feet like a fever, the kitchen walls began to shudder and shift, and we all fell in love with each other.

Very soon we'd be wedged, tight-crammed, in the window, waving our cups for more, while our Mother, bright-eyed, would be mumbling gaily:

'Lord bless you, Granny. Fancy cowsnips and parsney. You must give me the receipt, my dear.'

Granny Wallon would empty the jug in our cups, shake out the last drops on the flowers, then trot off tittering down the garden path, leaving us hugging ourselves in the window.

George Meredith

The nineteenth-century novelist and poet George Meredith fell from fashion long ago, yet in his time was a major figure of English literature, ranked with Hardy, and above Dickens, Thackeray and the rest. He was also a connoisseur of wine and wrote some fetching – indeed, luscious – descriptions of it in his novels. For example, on Veuve Clicqot: 'a champagne – rose-topaz in colour – of sober sweetness, of a great age. Counting up to the extreme maturity attained by wines of stilly depths – and their worthy comrade despite the wanton sparkles which in the Marriage with Time had extracted a spice of individuality from the saccharine.'

Champagne in general was evidently much enjoyed by Meredith, who thought that it 'presents us with a sphere for the pursuit of the thing we covet most … Philosophers partaking of it are drawn by the arms of garlanded nymphs about their necks into the fathomless of inquiries.'

He is at his most eloquent – which is saying a great deal – on the subject of wine in his novel, *The Egoist*. One of the most engaging characters is Dr Middleton, a clergyman of the utmost probity but with a weakness for vintage port. In the course of the story it is revealed he is more than ready to risk the happiness of his daughter for the privilege of sampling 90-year-old port from her suitor's wonderful cellar.

Burgundy was also favoured by the good doctor, who declared, 'Burgundy has great genius'. In *One of Our Conquerors*, one character asks another, 'What is your word on burgundy?' 'Our Falernian' is the thoroughly approved response.

G K Chesterton was a great admirer of Meredith, visiting him at his home at Box Hill when the author was very old. He told Chesterton that he had grown to enjoy ginger beer 'quite as much as champagne' – though whether this was a result of infirmity or the wisdom of age is not known.

The Egoist

A chirrup was in the Rev. Doctor's tone: 'Hocks, too, have compassed age. I have tasted senior Hocks. Their flavours are as a brook of many voices; they have depth also. Senatorial Port! we say. We cannot say that of any other wine. Port is deep-sea deep. It is in its flavour deep; mark the difference. It is like a classic tragedy, organic in conception. An ancient Hermitage has the light of the antique; the merit that it can grow to an extreme old age; a merit. Neither of Hermitage nor of Hock can you say that it is the blood of those long years, retaining the strength of youth with the wisdom of age. To Port for that! Port is our noblest legacy! Observe, I do not compare the wines; I distinguish the qualities. Let them live together for our enrichment; they are not rivals like the Idaean Three. Were they rivals, a fourth would challenge them. Burgundy has great genius. It does wonders within its period; it does all except to keep up in the race; it is short-lived. And aged Burgundy runs with a beardless Port. I cherish the fancy that Port speaks the sentences of wisdom, Burgundy sings the inspired Ode. Or put it, that Port is the Homeric hexameter, Burgundy the Pindaric dithyramb. What do you say?'

... Vernon and De Craye retired upon the arrival of the wine; and Dr Middleton sipped. He sipped and looked at the owner of it.

'Some thirty dozen?' he said.

'Fifty.'

'I shall remember, sir,' his host addressed him 'whenever I have the honour of entertaining you, I am cellarer of that wine.'

The Rev. Doctor set down his glass. 'You have, sir, in some sense, an enviable post. It is a responsible one, if that be a blessing. On you it devolves to retard the day of the last dozen.'

'Your opinion of the wine is favourable, sir?'

'I will say this: – shallow souls run to rhapsody; – I will say that I am consoled for not having lived ninety years back or at any period but the present, by this one glass of your ancestral wine.'

'I am careful of it,' Sir Willoughby said modestly: 'still its natural destination is to those who can appreciate it. You do, sir.'

'Still, my good friend, still. It is a charge; it is a possession, but part in trusteeship. Though we cannot declare it an entailed estate, our consciences are in some sort pledged that it shall be a succession not too considerably diminished.'

'You will not object to drink it, sir, to the health of your grandchildren. And may you live to toast them in it on their marriage-day!'

'You colour the idea of a prolonged existence in seductive hues. Ha! It is wine for Tithonus. This wine would speed him to the rosy Morning – aha!'

'I will undertake to sit you through it up to morning,' said Sir Willoughby, innocent of the Bacchic nuptiality of the allusion.

Dr Middleton eyed the decanter. There is a grief in gladness, for a premonition of our mortal state. The amount of wine in the decanter did not promise to sustain the starry roof of night and greet the dawn. 'Old wine, my friend denies us the full bottle!'

'Another bottle is to follow.'

'No!'

'It is ordered.'

'I protest.'

'It is uncorked.'

'I entreat.'

'It is decanted.'

'I submit. But, mark, it must be honest partnership. You are my worthy host, sir, on that stipulation. Note the superiority of wine over Venus! – I may say, the magnanimity of wine; our jealousy turns on him that will not share! But the corks, Willoughby. The corks excite my amazement.'

'The corking is examined at regular intervals. I remember the occurrence in my father's time. I have seen to it once.'

'It must be perilous as an operation for tracheotomy; which I should assume it to resemble in surgical skill and firmness of hand, not to mention the imminent gasp of the patient.'

A fresh decanter was placed before the doctor.

He said: 'I have but a girl to give!' He was melted.

Sir Willoughby replied: 'I take her for the highest prize this world affords.'

Walter Scott

Best remembered for a series of now largely unread historical novels (*Waverley*, *Ivanhoe*, *Guy Mannering*, and so on), Scott has become a venerated historical figure in the annals of Scotland, a fitting subject for marble busts and worthy biographies. In his time, however, he was quite a hell-raiser, drinking in the manner expected of a Scottish gentleman: that is, above all else, heavily.

In his work as an advocate he was admired as much for his ability to take large quantities of drink without becoming roaring drunk as for his skill in legal matters. Drunk or sober, it was said, he was aye the gentleman.

As a young man he lived a roistering life in the Scottish Borders. The day would be enlivened by the arrival of a keg of smuggled brandy from the shores of the Solway, whisky punch was drunk from milk pails and breakfast would consist of devilled ducks and pints of porter. In later life he suffered from stomach troubles which he attributed to earlier drinking excesses, but, according to his first biographer, Lockhart:

> In truth he liked no wine except sparkling Champagne and Claret; but even as to this last he was no connoisseur, and sincerely preferred a tumbler of whisky-toddy to the most precious liquid ruby that ever flowed in the cup of a prince. He rarely took any other potation when alone with his family; but at the Sunday board he circulated the Champagne briskly during dinner and considered a pint of Claret each man's fair share afterwards.

And this, it should be remembered, was when Scotland had stocks of the finest clarets, shipped direct from Bordeaux to the port of Leith

Peveril of the Peak

> The Duke threw himself into a chair, fixed his eye on the ground, and spoke without raising them: 'I am about to call Jerningham', he said; 'but fear nothing – it is only for a draught of wine. The stuff on the table may be a vehicle for filberts and walnuts but not for communications such as yours.'
>
> 'Bring me Champagne', he said to the attendant who answered his summons. The domestic returned and brought a flask of Champagne.

Anthony Trollope

Anthony Trollope

The private life of Trollope was very much the same as the public life of Trollope, senior civil servant, or that of Trollope, the author. He was a typical Victorian gentleman with the tastes typical of a man of his class: winin' and dinin' and drinkin'. He was a gregarious, clubbable man, fond of wine, cigars and good company.

But he was untypical in his energy and talent. Apart from producing a string of fat and highly successful novels, he was a capable and competent civil servant (he worked for the Post Office for more than thirty years and was the inventor of the pillar box) and a busy, prolific journalist.

Trollope's feelings for wine are reflected in his books. In *The American Senator* he almost winces at the lack of appreciation shown to a '57 Mouton and confides, 'I – who write this – have seen myself an honoured guest deluge with the pump the most hard earned, most scarce and peculiar vintage.'

His personal favourite among clarets was the '64 Leoville, 'the most divine of nectars'. Given his partiality to this wine, his generosity in making a gift of it to his son is even more remarkable. In January 1882 he wrote a courteous note to his son about the contents of his cellar: 'I wish you to consider the two bin ends at the further end as your own. They contain Leoville and Beychevelle. They are at present two dozen of each. It is 1864 and they will not be fit for use until 1884. Should I take a few bottles for use I hope you will pardon the intrusion.' The tone is magnificent and a sad reminder that few of us have been blessed with fathers of such taste and capable of such nobility.

Trollope was something of a pioneer in taking an interest in New World wines during his travels to America and Australia. He was not as impressed by the wines of Australia as connoisseurs are today (not surprising in a man with a feeling for fine claret) but he thought the best came from South Australia with the wines from Yering on the Upper Yarra being 'both wholesome and nutritive'.

The Prime Minister

Mrs. Roby had secured a lord, – an absolute peer of Parliament! This was no less a man than Lord Mongrober whose father had been a great judge in the early part of the century, and had been made a peer. The Mongrober estates were not supposed to be large, nor was the Mongrober influence at this time extensive. But this nobleman was seen about a good deal in society when the dinners given were supposed to be worth eating. He was a fat, silent, red-faced, elderly gentleman, who said very little, and who when he did speak seemed always to be in an ill-humour. He would now and then make ill-natured remarks about his friends' wines, as suggesting '68 when a man would boast of his '48 claret; and when costly dainties were supplied for his use, would remark that such and such a dish was very well at some other time of the year. So that ladies attentive to their tables and hosts proud of their cellars would almost shake in their shoes before Lord Mongrober. And it may also be said that Lord Mongrober never gave any chance of retaliation by return dinners. There lived not the man or woman who had dined with Lord Mongrober …

'You remember that claret, my lord?' said Dick, thinking that some little compensation was due to him for what had been said about the champagne.

But Lord Mongrober's dinner had not yet had the effect of mollifying the man sufficiently for Dick's purposes. 'Oh, yes, I remember the wine. You call it '57, don't you?'

'And it is '57 – '57, Leoville.'

'Very likely, – very likely. If it hadn't been heated before the fire—'

'It hasn't been near the fire,' said Dick.

'Or put into a hot decanter—'

'Nothing of the kind.'

'Or treated after some other damnable fashion, it would be very good wine, I dare say.'

'You are hard to please, my lord, to-day,' said Dick, who was put beyond his bearing.

'What is a man to say? If you will talk about your wine I can only tell you what I think. Any man may get good wine, – that is if he can afford to pay the price, – but it isn't one out of ten who knows how to put it on the table.' Dick felt this to be very hard. When a man pays 110s. a dozen for his champagne, and then gives it to guests like Lord Mongrober who are not even expected to return the favour, then that man ought to be allowed to talk about his wine without fear of rebuke. One doesn't have an agreement to that effect written down on parchment and sealed; but it is as well understood and ought to be as faithfully kept as any legal contract. Dick, who could on occasion be awakened to a touch of manliness, gave the bottle a shove and threw himself back in his chair. 'If you ask me, I can only tell you,' repeated Lord Mongrober.

'I don't believe you ever had a bottle of wine put before you in better order in all your life,' said Dick. His lordship's face became very square and very red as he looked round at his host. 'And as for talking about my wine, of course I talk to a man about what he understands. I talk to Monogram about pigeons, to Tom there about politics, to 'Apperton and Lopez about the price of consols, and to you about wine. If I asked you what you thought of the last new book, your lordship would be a little surprised.' Lord Mongrober grunted and looked redder and squarer than ever; but he made no attempt at reply, and the victory was evidently left with Dick, – very much to the general exaltation of his character. And he was proud of himself. 'We had a little tiff, me and Mongrober,' he said to his wife that night. ' 'E's a very good fellow, and of course he's a lord and all that. But he has to be put down occasionally, and, by George, I did it to-night. You ask Lopez.'

Pubs, Clubs, Bars and Various Drinking Dens

There hath been great sale and utterance of wine,
Besides beer, and ale, and ipocras fine,
In every country region and nation.

Anon, sixteenth century

Simone de Beauvoir

Simone de Beauvoir's intensely industrious approach to her work when a student led her to being christened 'beaver' (*castor*, in French); because she beavered away at her studies. It is interesting to speculate what she might have been called if her drinking habits had been the source of the nickname: Le Grand Soif, perhaps, or Votre Santé or Encore.

The fact that she drank heavily is surprising because her works are so cerebral that she hardly seems to belong to the world of drinking sessions and hangovers known to most normal beings. Another cause for surprise, if not astonishment, is how she managed to live a life so rich in lovers, male and female, to be one of the great writers of her day, a leading intellectual and philosopher, while putting away enough drink to knock out even the most seasoned sozzler.

Small, neat, precise, formidable, she was an indefatigable party-goer. In the period just after World War II, Paris was on the spree. Parties would end with bodies strewn all over the place but Simone would be as neat and controlled as at the beginning – and bright eyed and bushy tailed the next day. She would have had some justification for calling her great work *The Superior Sex*, because that is what she was.

Scotch whisky was her favoured tipple, a taste she had developed in the postwar years in France. According to the excellent biography by Deirdre Bair, de Beavoir admitted in 1982, 'I like to drink very much ... it has become for me an element of equilibrium. I mean, I feel better when I drink something before lunch and then in the afternoon I have two or three Scotches during the day.'

The glasses drunk were very large. She didn't care for wine – though she drank plenty on occasions – but preferred strong drink. Indeed, she thought vodka and Scotch 'necessary' for her but claimed she no longer had any desire to get drunk: 'Well, it was fun just after the war, when everyone got drunk. But I don't do that any more. However, the drinking I do in the day and evening – that, for me, is essential. I need that.' Bottles of Scotch and vodka were stacked in the fridge at her apartment, ready for her to start the day with vodka before going to Johnny Walker Red later on.

Her great soulmate and partner, Sartre, also drank heavily, and they enjoyed many bibulous sessions, both in public and in private. Sartre had a remarkable appetite for food and drink – huge meals with lashings of red wine and rich desserts, tea, coffee and barbiturates to help him keep working.

Towards the end of her life, when she was close to death with cirrhosis of the liver, she refused to give up vodka and Scotch, despite the warnings of doctors, saying that she would rather maintain her chosen way of life.

The Prime of Life

> To begin with, we let rip on the food and drink. Every fête plays havoc with one's normal economy for the sake of a real blowout; and so, at a modest level, it was with us. It required great care and severe self-restraint to amass the provisions and bottles with which we stacked the buffet; then, suddenly, we found ourselves eating and drinking all we could put away. Abundance, so nauseating when cultivated for the mere show of the thing – I am thinking, for instance, of the picnic I went on with Zaza, along the bank of the Adour River – becomes a most stirring affair when it caters to famished stomachs. We stayed our pangs of hunger with shameless zest. Casual love-making played a very small part in these revels. It was, primarily, drink which aided our break with the daily humdrum round; when it came to alcohol, we never held back, and none of us had any objections to getting drunk. Some even regarded it as a duty. Leiris, among others, set about the task enthusiastically and made a most admirable job of it. I can see him now, bumping down the staircase on his bottom, a hilarious expression on his face as he bounded from step to step, yet never losing his somewhat formally dignified appearance. Each of us turned himself, more or less deliberately, into some sort of clown for the others' benefit, and there was no shortage of special attractions: we constituted a sort of carnival, with its mountebanks, its confidence-men, its clowns, and its parades. Dora Marr used to mime a bullfighting act; Limbour carved up a ham as though he were a cannibal; Queneau and Bataille fought a

duel with bottles instead of swords; Camus and Lemarchand played military marches on saucepan lids, while those who knew how to sing, sang. So did those who didn't. We had pantomimes, comedies, diatribes, parodies, monologues and confessions: the flow of improvisations never dried up, and they were always greeted with enthusiastic applause. We put on records and danced; some of us, such as Olga, Wanda, and Camus, very well; others less expertly. Filled with the joy of living, I regained my old conviction that life both can and ought to be a real pleasure. This belief would last into the quiet dawn hours; then it would fade (though it never completely died) and the waiting began again.

We went to La Pueze for Easter. During our absence Paris was bombed almost every night.

Samuel Beckett

Beckett's work has been described as a grim joke about the absurdity of existence but the real joke may be that Beckett himself, although notorious for his pessimism, enjoyed a life that was far from bleak. He may have had a deep streak of melancholy but he thoroughly enjoyed his fair share of the good things of life, mainly drink and sex.

His appearance – the bony, eagle face, the searching eyes – made him appear a natural ascetic. He looked just as the author of *Waiting for Godot*, *Endgame* and other works should look: stripped of vanity, of any excess, relentless in the pursuit of truth. The stories about his bleakness of vision are legion, although many may be apocryphal, such as the one where he was walking with a friend on a beautiful summer's day in London.

'Ah, Sam, there are times when it feels grand to be alive,' said the friend.

'Well, I wouldn't go quite as far as that,' said Beckett.

As a young man in Paris, Beckett became part of the circle around James Joyce, acting as a kind of secretary. Beckett revered Joyce, who had a great influence on his writing and, probably, his drinking habits.

Joyce was highly sociable and enjoyed the long nights in the cafés of Paris. When asked why he did not appear in a famous photograph of Joyce and his cronies, Beckett replied that he was probably there, but under the table.

Samuel Beckett and
Simone de Beauvoir
LET'S GO.
WE CAN'T.
WHY NOT?
WE'RE WAITING
FOR A REFILL.

His official biographer, James Knowlson, says Beckett rarely drank before five in the afternoon, although there is plenty of evidence that he broke the rule on a number of occasions. It is also clear that when he did drink, he did so with enthusiasm.

In Paris he drank Chambertin but preferred dry white wines, perhaps influenced by the master, Joyce, whose taste lay in that direction. He also sampled an extraordinary mixture of Fernet-Branca and port, undoubtedly out of loyalty to Joyce who was known to offer this dubious cocktail to unfortunate guests. In Ireland the principal drinks were much more normal, stout and whiskey, John Jameson being a favourite brand, which was also part of his daily life in Paris. Iconoclastic in literary matters, he was quite conventional in some aspects of his drinking – for example, he followed the eighteenth-century practice of taking copious amounts of champagne when involved in sexual affairs.

Beckett was a pretty hard drinker all his life but never a drunk, although he was, naturally enough, often drunk. He had some tremendous sessions ('late and lubricated nights') when rehearsing his plays in London, particularly with the Irish actors Patrick Magee and Jack MacGowran, both brilliant Beckett performers and notoriously hard-drinking men.

Murphy

> With regard to the disposal of these my body, mind and soul, I desire that they be burnt and placed in a paper bag and brought to the Abbey Theatre, Lr. Abbey Street, Dublin, and without pause into what the great and good Lord Chesterfield calls the necessary house, where their happiest hours have been spent, on the right as one goes down into the pit, and I desire that the chain be there pulled upon them, if possible during the performance of a piece, the whole to be executed without ceremony or show of grief.
>
> … [Cooper] got away from the Mercyseat with the parcel of ash under his arm. It must have weighed well on four pounds. Various ways of getting rid of it suggested themselves to him on the way to the station. Finally he decided that the most convenient and inconspicuous was to drop it in the first receptacle for refuse that he came to. In Dublin he need only have sat down on

the nearest bench and waited. Soon one of the gloomy dustmen would have come, wheeling his cart marked, 'Post your litter here'. But London was less conscious of her garbage, she had not given her scavenging to aliens.

He was turning into the station, without having met any considerable receptacle for refuse, when a burst of music made him halt and turn. It was the pub across the way, opening for the evening session. The lights sprang up in the saloon, the doors burst open, the radio struck up. He crossed the street and stood on the threshold. The floor was palest ochre, the pin-tables shone like silver, the quoits board had a net, the stools the high rungs that he loved, the whiskey was in glass tanks, a slow cascando of pellucid yellows. A man brushed past him into the saloon, one of the million that had been wanting a drink for the past two hours. Cooper followed slowly and sat down at the bar, for the first time in more than twenty years.

'What are you taking, friend?' said the man.

'The first is mine,' said Cooper, his voice trembling.

Some hours later Cooper took the packet of ash from his pocket, where earlier in the evening he had put it for greater security, and threw it angrily at a man who had given him great offence. It bounced, burst, off the wall on to the floor, where at once it became the object of much dribbling, passing, trapping, shooting, punching, heading and even some recognition from the gentleman's code. By closing time the body, mind and soul of Murphy were freely distributed over the floor of the saloon; and before another dayspring greyened the earth had been swept away with the sand, the beer, the butts, the glass, the matches, the spits, the vomit.

Hilaire Belloc

There are any number of Bellocs in the substantial persona that was Hilaire Belloc. Two of the most familiar are apparently contradictory: Hilaire Belloc as Sussex countryman, supping ale in mellow age with companions from boyhood, and Hilaire Belloc, proud, passionate Frenchman with accent to match, lover of fine food and fine wine. The odd thing is that both are true pictures. His father was French, his mother English, and he was naturally drawn to the culture of both countries.

He lived in an age of hard drinking when great literary men disputed loudly and publicly in bars, restaurants and private houses. El Vino's in Fleet Street was a favoured haunt where Belloc's great friend, G K Chesterton, held court and was often joined by Belloc who, in the words of Christopher Hollis 'might rush in like a nor'easter'. Once arrived he would immediately become embroiled in pugnacious dispute, shouting and drinking, to the delight of other customers. He was often compared to a storm, a hurricane or tornado as he swept through London, Sussex and France, lavishly entertaining scores of friends with the best wines and food, enjoying what may have been his greatest passion, talking.

Belloc's character was formed early. At Oxford he was noisy, loud, drunken, brilliant, an unforgettable figure in large cape and black hat – as he was to dress for the rest of his life. He captured these days in poetry:

> We kept the Rabelaisian plan:
> We dignified the dainty cloisters
> With Natural Law, the Rights of Man,
> Song, Stoicism, Wine and Oysters.

There were rowdy parties: syphons thrown about, food stuck to the ceiling, port drunk and thrown about – a contemporary records that there was even a special brand of port which was called throwing port.

It is safe to assume that Belloc in later life drank more port than he wasted. He certainly maintained a deep interest in wine throughout his life. He was ever ready to give advice on the subject: warning that red wine should never be warmed and giving an idiosyncratic method of drawing the corks of fizzy wines: 'The rule is to take a sharp knife and cut off the excrescence leaving the rest of the cork flush with the top of the bottle. Then pull it out as you would an ordinary cork.'

It is a little ironic that this man of many parts, prolific in all of them – novelist, poet, essayist, politician, historian and journalist – should be remembered today principally for his light or comic verse written for children. Yet it was hugely successful in his day and can still raise a smile, as is witnessed in these lines:

And yet I really must complain
About the Company's Champagne!
This most expensive kind of wine
In England is a matter
Of pride or habit when we dine
(Presumably the latter)
Beneath an equatorial sky
And stern, indomitable men
Have told me, time and time again,
'The nuisance of the tropics is
The sheer necessity of fizz'.

Belloc's affection for wine remained until his death. He had described it poetically as 'Strong brother in God and last companion, wine'. As he died in the summer of 1953 at the age of 83 his lines came true when he was permitted a final glass of wine.

The Path to Rome

We went up the hill together over a burnt land, but shaded with trees. It was very hot, I could scarcely continue, so fast did my companion go, and so much did the heat oppress me.

We passed a fountain at which oxen drank, and there I supped up cool water from the spout, but he wagged his finger before his face to tell me that this was an error under a hot sun.

We went on and met two men driving cattle up the path between the trees. These I soon found to be talking of prices and markets with my guide. For it was market-day. As we came up at last on to the little town – a little, little town like a nest, and all surrounded with walls, and a castle in it and a church – we found a thousand beasts all lowing and answering each other along the highroad, and on into the market square through the gate. There my guide led me into a large room, where a great many peasants were eating soup with macaroni in it, and some few, meat. But I was too exhausted to eat meat, so I supped up my broth and then began diapephradizing on my fingers to show the great innkeeper what I wanted.

I first pulled up the macaroni out of the dish, and said, *Fromagio, Pommodoro*, by which I meant cheese – tomato. He then said he knew what I meant and brought me that spaghetti so treated, which is a dish for a king, a cosmopolitan traitor, an oppressor of the poor, a usurer, or any other rich man, but there is no spaghetti in the place which such men go, whereas these peasants will continue to enjoy it in heaven.

I then pulled out my bottle of wine, drank what was left out of the neck (by way of sign), and putting it down said, '*Tale, tantum, vino rosso*'. My guide also said many things which probably meant that I was a rich man, who threw his money about by the sixpence. So the innkeeper went through a door and brought back a bottle all corked and sealed, and said on his fingers, and with his mouth and eyes, 'THIS KIND OF WINE IS SOMETHING VERY SPECIAL'.

Only in the foolish cities do men think it a fine thing to appear careless of money. So I, very narrowly watching him out of half-closed eyes, held up my five fingers interrogatively, and said, '*Cinquante*?' meaning 'Dare you ask fivepence?'

At which he and all the peasants around, even including my guide, laughed aloud as at an excellent joke, and said, '*Cinquante, Ho! Ho!*' and dug each other in the ribs. But the innkeeper of Tizzano Val Permense said in Italian a number of things which meant that I could but be joking, and added (in passing) that a lira made it a kind of gift to me. A lira was, as it were, but a token to prove that it had changed hands: a registration fee: a matter of record; at a lira it was pure charity. Then I said '*Soixante Dix*?' which meant nothing to him, so I held up seven fingers; he waved his hand about genially and said that as I was evidently a good fellow, a traveller, and as anyhow he was practically giving me the wine, he would make it ninepence; it was hardly worth his while to stretch out his hand for so little money. So then I pulled out 80c. in coppers, and said '*Tutto*' which means 'all'. Then he put the bottle before me, took the money and an immense clamour rose from all those who had been watching the scene, and they applauded it as a ratified bargain. And this is the way in which bargains were struck of old time in these hills when your fathers and mine lived and shivered in a cave, hunted wolves, and bargained with clubs only.

So this being settled, and I eager for the wine, wished it to be opened, especially to stand drink to my guide. The innkeeper was in another room. The guide was too courteous to ask for a corkscrew, and I did not know the Italian for corkscrew.

I pointed to the cork, but all I got out of my guide was a remark that the wine was very good. Then I made the emblem and sign of a corkscrew in my sketch-book with a pencil, but he pretended not to understand – such was his breeding. Then I imitated the mode, sound and gesture of a corkscrew entering a cork, and an old man next to me said '*Tire-buchon*' – a common French word as familiar as the woods of Marly! It was brought. The bottle was opened and we all drank together.

As I rose to go out of Tizzano Val Parmense my guide said to me, '*Se chiama Tira-Buchon perche E' tira il buchon*'. And I said to him '*Dominus Vobiscum*' and left him to his hills.

Thomas Hardy

The image of Thomas Hardy that looms across the years is melancholy, introspective, immensely respectable, hypersensitive, far removed from simple human pleasures such as drinking. But Hardy was a countryman, a rural lad who was thoroughly familiar with country pleasures. His native village of Puddletown on the River Piddle was notorious for drunkenness. A local rhyme describes a Puddletown Sunday and the relative attractions of the church and the Old Cat pub:

Into church
Out of Church
Into Cat Out of Cat,
Into Piddle.

His father was an amateur fiddler, much in demand at dances and fairs. Young Hardy followed in his father's footsteps, playing with him at festivities around the county. These occasions often developed into wild affairs with heavy drinking and uninhibited, virtually public lovemaking. It is true Hardy – a deeply secretive man about his life and habits – does not describe these less than decorous affairs but there are echoes of his music-making youth in some of his verse:

The dance it is a great thing,
A great thing to me,

With candles lit and partners fit
For night-long revelry;
And going home when day-dawning
Peeps pale upon the lea.

There was a tradition of smugglers coming up from the coast with contraband to be stored and some left as a reward. One of the legendary figures of his childhood was a huge woman known as Mother Rogers who would call on the villagers offering cheap spirits. She was vast because of animals' bladders full of spirit which she carried on her hips. These memories surface in his stories, such as *The Distracted Preacher*.

Jude Fawley in *Jude the Obscure* was partly modelled on a relation, John Antell, married to his Aunt Mary who also lived in Puddletown. He was a cobbler, intelligent enough to have taught himself Latin but something of a drunkard.

London in the latter half of the nineteenth century, when Hardy was working there in an architectural practice, while superficially respectable, had a very seamy side. Thousands of prostitutes roamed the streets and pleasure gardens. Hardy was a young man, visiting the opera, museums, art galleries and less educational places such as the Cider Cellars in Leicester Square where raffish entertainment was available.

When ill he recovered in Dorset, taking a prescribed bottle of stout a day. The 'bitter ales of Bass and Allsop' were also recommended. And it is certain he sampled the 'sweet cyder' of Dorset that he remembered so fondly in his poems. The cider-making described in his novel *Desperate Remedies* has the authentic flavour of personal observation.

The Distracted Preacher

He had finished supper, and was not in the least anticipating Mrs Newberry again that night, when she tapped and entered as before. Stockdale's gratified look told that she had lost nothing by not appearing when expected. It happened that the cold in the head from which the young man suffered had increased with the approach of night, and before she had spoken he was seized with a violent fit of sneezing which he could not anyhow repress.

Mrs Newberry looked full of pity. 'Your cold is very bad tonight, Mr Stockdale.'

Stockdale replied that it was rather troublesome.

'And I've a good mind—' she added archly, looking at the cheerless glass of water on the table, which the abstemious minister was going to drink.

'Yes, Mrs Newberry?'

'I've a good mind that you should have something more likely to cure it than that cold stuff.'

'Well,' said Stockdale, looking down at the glass, 'as there is no inn here and nothing better to be got in the village, of course it will do.'

To this she replied, 'There is something better, not far off, though not in the house. I really think you must try it, or you may be ill. Yes, Mr Stockdale, you shall.' She held up her finger, seeing that he was about to speak. 'Don't ask what it is; wait, and you shall see.'

Then from under her cloak she produced a small lighted lantern which the minister had not noticed that she carried at all. The light showed them to be close to the singing-gallery stairs, under which lay a heap of lumber of all sorts, but consisting most of decayed framework, pews, panels, and pieces of flooring, that from time to time had been removed from their original fixings in the body of the edifice and replaced by new.

'Perhaps you will drag some of those boards aside?' she said, holding the lantern over her head to light him better. 'Or will you take the lantern while I move them?'

'I can manage it,' said the young man, and acting as she ordered, he uncovered, to his surprise, a row of little barrels bound with wood hoops, each barrel being about as large as the nave of a heavy waggon-wheel. When they were laid open Lizzy fixed her eyes on him, as if she wondered what he would say.

'You know what they are?' she asked, finding that he did not speak.

'Yes, barrels,' said Stockdale simply. He was an inland man, the son of highly respectable parents, and brought up with a single eye to the ministry; and the sight suggested nothing beyond the fact that such articles were there.

'You are quite right, they are barrels,' she said, in an emphatic tone of candour that was not without a touch of irony.

Stockdale looked at her with an eye of sudden misgiving. 'Not smugglers' liquor?' he said.

'Yes,' said she. 'They are tubs of spirit that have accidentally floated over in the dark from France.'

In Nether-Moynton and its vicinity at this date people always smiled at the sort of sin called in the outside world illicit trading; and these little kegs of gin and brandy were as well known to the inhabitants as turnips. So that Stockdale's innocent ignorance, and his look of alarm when he guessed the sinister mystery, seemed to strike Lizzy first as ludicrous, and then as very awkward for the good impression that she wished to produce upon him.

'Smuggling is carried on here by some of the people,' she said in a gentle apologetic voice. 'It has been their practice for generations, and they think it no harm. Now, will you roll out one of the tubs?'

'What to do with it?'

'To draw a little from it to cure your cold,' she answered. 'It is so 'nation strong that it drives away that sort of thing in a jiffy. O, it is all right about our taking it. I may have what I like; the owner of the tubs says so. I ought to have had some in the house, and then I shouldn't ha' been put to this trouble; but I drink none myself, and so I often forget to keep it indoors.'

'You are allowed to help yourself, I suppose, that you may not inform where their hiding-place is?'

'Well, no; not that particularly; but I may take any if I want it. So help yourself.'

'I will, to oblige you, since you have a right to it,' murmured the minister; and though he was not quite satisfied with his part in the performance, he rolled one of the 'tubs' out from the corner into the middle of the tower floor. 'How do you wish me to get it out – with a gimlet, I suppose?'

'No, I'll show you,' said his interesting companion; and she held up with her other hand a shoemaker's awl and a hammer. 'You must never do these things with a gimlet, because the wood-dust gets in; and when the buyers pour out the brandy that would tell them that the tub had been broached. An awl makes no dust, and the hole nearly closes up again. Now tap one of the hoops forward.'

Stockdale took the hammer and did so.

'Now make the hole in the part that was covered by the hoop.'

He made the hole as directed. 'It won't run out,' he said.

'O yes it will,' said she. 'Take the tub between your knees, and squeeze the heads; and I'll hold the cup.'

Stockdale obeyed; and the pressure taking effect upon the tub, which seemed to be thin, the spirit spirted out in a stream. When the cup was full he ceased pressing, and the flow immediately stopped. 'Now we must fill up the keg with water,' said Lizzy, 'or it will cluck like forty hens when it is handled, and show that 'tis not full.'

'But they tell you you may take it?'

'Yes, the *smugglers*; but the *buyers* must not know that the smugglers have been kind to me at their expense.'

Jerome K Jerome

From the evidence of his books, not only his official autobiography, *My Life and Times*, but the autobiographical *Three Men in a Boat*, it is clear Jerome K Jerome was a sensible drinker rather than a sot.

On the much-neglected art of learning how to drink, Jerome takes issue with Dr Johnson and his famous remarks about port being a drink for men, saying he would advise any boy of his to start straight away on port. As a young man he had begun with claret at 2½*d* a glass which he forced down with his eyes shut. He then tried porter which tasted even worse. At last he found port – three pence a glass with a large bun thrown in – and began to enjoy drink. From port, he worked his way through to bottled beer and even to whisky.

In his Victorian youth, drinking was a necessary skill:

> For recreation young bloods of an evening would gather together in groups and do a mouch 'round the houses'. To be on a footing of familiarity with a barmaid was the height of most young clerks' ambition. Failing that, to be entitled to address the potboy by his Christian name conferred distinction.

Many of Jerome's friends were port lovers. He described the writer George Sala as a connoisseur. Sala was the owner of a remarkable nose about which, like Cyrano de Bergerac, he was rather touchy. He even brought a libel action against someone who had spoken disrespectfully of it.

Although known mainly as a humorist, especially after the success of *Three Men in a Boat*, Jerome was a successful playwright. He knew all the leading theatre people of the day, including Henry Irving who held first-night suppers on the stage, informal affairs at which the visitor simply showed his card and was wined and dined. In fact, he knew everybody in the literary world and was particularly friendly with Shaw, Wells, Doyle and Barrie.

He remembered the West End of horse-drawn carriages and gaslight, of Soho as the home of revolutionaries, of seeing (and pretending not to see) Oscar Wilde with a group of young friends at restaurants such as the Florence (dinner for two shillings) in Rupert Street.

Jerome's *Three Men on the Bummel* was a major success in Germany, even becoming a school textbook. He lived there for a time before the First World War and had fond memories of its people and of German beer. The trouble with it, he said, was that it did not go to the head, with the result that one never knew when one had had enough.

He recalled especially the product of a brewery near Munich which was noted for the quality of its beer. He, his children and their governess attended a beer garden to sample the brew.

> Our governess, who was from Dresden, said 'Be careful'. She had heard about this beer. I claim that I was careful. The girls had each one mug. I explained to them that this was not the ordinary beer they were used to; and that anyhow they were not going to have any more. It was a warm afternoon. They answered haughtily and drank it off. Our governess, a sweet, high-minded lady – I cannot conceive of her having done anything wrong in all her life – had one and part of another. I myself, on the principle of safety first, had decided to limit myself to three. I was toying with the third when my eldest girl, saying she wanted to go home, suddenly got up, turned round and sat down again. The younger swept a glass from the table to make room for her head, gave a sigh of contentment and went to sleep. I looked at Frau Lankau.
>
> 'Whatever we do,' she said, 'we must avoid attracting attention. You remain here, as though nothing had happened. I will lead the poor dears away, and find the carriage. A little later, you will follow quietly.'

I could not have thought of anything more sensible myself. She gathered her things together and rose. The following moment she sat down again: it was really one and the same movement.

The dilemma ended with the arrival of a muscular gentleman, whose job it was to help customers in difficulties for a small fee, who escorted the party back to their carriage.

Three Men in a Boat

'We shan't want any tea,' said George (Harris's face fell at this); 'but we'll have a good round, square, slap-up meal at seven – dinner, tea, and supper combined.'

Harris grew more cheerful. George suggested meat and fruit pies, cold meat, tomatoes, fruit and green stuff. For drink, we took some wonderful sticky concoction of Harris's, which you mixed with water and called lemonade, plenty of tea, and a bottle of whisky, in case, as George said, we got upset.

It seemed to me that George harped too much on the getting-upset idea. It seemed to me the wrong spirit to go about the trip in.

But I'm glad we took the whisky.

We didn't take beer or wine. They are a mistake up the river. They make you feel sleepy and heavy. A glass in the evening when you are doing a mooch round the town and looking at the girls is right enough; but don't drink when the sun is blazing down on your head, and you've got hard work to do …

Caesar, like in later years, Elizabeth, seems to have stopped everywhere; only he was more respectable than good queen Bess; he didn't put up at the public-houses.

She was nuts on public-houses, was England's Virgin Queen. There's scarcely a pub of any attractions within ten miles of London that she does not seem to have looked in at, or stopped at, or slept at, some time or other. I wonder now, supposing Harris, say, turned over a new leaf, and became a great and good man, and got to be Prime Minister, and died, if they would put up signs over the public houses that he had patronised: 'Harris had a glass of bitter in this house'; 'Harris had two of Scotch cold here in the summer of '88'; 'Harris was chucked from here in December 1886'.

No, there would be too many of them! It would be the houses that he had never entered that would become famous. 'Only house in South London that Harris never had a drink in!' The people would flock to it to see what could have been the matter with it …

'I'm going to get out, and have a drink.'

I pointed out to him that we were miles away from a pub; and then he went on about the river, and what was the good of the river, and was everyone who came on the river to die of thirst?

It is always best to let Harris have his head when he gets like this. Then he pumps himself out, and is quiet afterwards.

I reminded him that there was concentrated lemonade in the hamper, and a gallon jar of water in the nose of the boat, and that the two only wanted mixing to make a cool and refreshing beverage.

Then he flew off about lemonade, and 'such-like Sunday school slops', as he termed them, ginger-beer, raspberry syrup, etc. etc. He said they all produced dyspepsia, and ruined body and soul alike, and were the cause of half the crime in England.

He said he must drink something, however, and climbed upon the seat, and leant over to get the bottle. It was right at the bottom of the hamper, and seemed difficult to find, and he had to lean over farther and farther, and, in trying to steer at the same time, from a topsy-turvy point of view, he pulled the wrong line, and sent the boat into the bank, and the shock upset him, and he dived down right into the hamper, and stood there on his head, holding on to the sides of the boat like grim death, his legs sticking up into the air. He dared not move for fear of going over, and had to stay there till I could get hold of his legs, and haul him back and that made him madder than ever …

From Picnic Point to Old Windsor lock is a delightful bit of the river. A shady road, dotted here and there with dainty little cottages, runs by the bank up to the 'Bells of Ouseley', a picturesque inn, as most up-river inns are, and a place where a very good glass of ale may be drunk – so Harris says; and on a matter of this kind you can take Harris's word.

Eugene O'Neill

Eugene O'Neill was an expert on drinking, from background and personal experience. Drink flowed in the family. His father and brothers were heavy drinkers and he became one as soon as he was able to do so. A poem by O'Neill from the period reflects his two chief interests, common to most young men:

> Cheeks that have known no rouge
> Lips that have known no booze
> What care I for thee?
> Come with me on a souse,
> A long and everlast carouse
> And I'll adore thee.

O'Neill launched himself on a series of drunken escapades and debauches, frequenting bars that were to form the basis of Harry Hope's Last Chance saloon in what some consider his greatest play, *The Iceman Cometh*. When money was short he would try to get by on beer but when in funds his favourite tipple was a big glass of gin with just a drop of vermouth and soda.

A contemporary described a familiar O'Neill routine in a way that is eerily reminiscent of Faulkner's account of Jiggs in *Python*.

> O'Neill would prop himself against the bar and order his shot. The bartender knew him, and would place the glass in front of him, toss a towel across the bar, as though absentmindedly forgetting it, and move away. Arranging the towel round his neck, O'Neill would grasp the glass of whiskey and an end of the towel in one hand and clutch the other end of the towel with his other hand. Using the towel as a pulley, he would laboriously hoist the glass to his lips. His hands trembled so violently that even with this aid he would scarcely pour the whiskey down his throat, and often spilled part of it.

O'Neill stopped drinking completely at the age of 37, which was just as well as no constitution could have survived his intake of alcohol, and lived to 65.

The Iceman Cometh

LARRY (*leans toward him, a comical intensity in his low voice*) Don't mock the faith! Have you no respect for religion, you unregenerate Wop? What's it matter if the truth is that their favouring breeze has the stink of nickel whisky on its breath, and their sea is a growler of lager and ale, and their ships are long since looted and scuttled and sunk on the bottom? To hell with the truth! As the history of the world proves, the truth has no bearing on anything. It's irrelevant and immaterial, as the lawyers say. The lie of a pipe dream is what gives life to the whole misbegotten mad lot of us, drunk or sober. And that's enough philosophic wisdom to give you for one drink of rot-gut …

It's not. Don't waste your pity. They wouldn't thank you for it. They manage to get drunk, by hook or crook, and keep their pipe dreams, and that's all they ask of life. I've never known more contented men. It isn't often that men attain the true goal of their heart's desire. The same applies to Harry himself and his two cronies at the far table. He's so satisfied with life he's never set foot out of this place since his wife died twenty years ago. He has no need of the outside world at all. This place has a fine trade from the Market people across the street and the waterfront workers, so in spite of Harry's thirst and his generous heart, he comes out even. He never worried in hard times because there's always old friends from the days when he was a jitney Tammany politician, and a friendly brewery to tide him over. Don't ask me what his two pals work at because they don't. Except at being his lifetime guests. The one facing this way is his brother-in-law, Ed Mosher, who once worked for a circus in the ticket wagon. Pat McGloin, the other one, was a police lieutenant back in the flush times of graft when everything went. But he got too greedy and when the usual reform investigation came he was caught red-handed and thrown off the Force. (*He nods at Joe*) Joe here has a yesterday in the same flush period. He ran a coloured gambling-house then and was a hell of a sport, so they say. Well, that's our whole family circle of inmates, except the two barkeeps and their girls, three ladies of the pavement that room on the third floor …

*

HICKEY (*grinning*) Oh, hell, Governor! You don't think I'd come around here peddling some brand of temperance bunk, do you? You know me better than that! Just because I'm through with the stuff don't mean I'm going Prohibition. Hell, I'm not that ungrateful! It's given me too many good times. I feel exactly the same as I always did. If anyone wants to get drunk, if that's the only way they can be happy, and feel at peace with themselves, why the hell shouldn't they? They have my full and entire sympathy. I know all about that game from soup to nuts. I'm the guy that wrote the book. The only reason I've quit is – Well, I finally had the guts to face myself and throw overboard the damned lying pipe dream that'd been making me miserable, and do what I had to do for the happiness of all concerned – and then all at once I found I was at peace with myself and I didn't need booze any more. That's all there was to it. (*He pauses. They are staring at him, uneasy and beginning to feel defensive. Hickey looks round and grins affectionately – apologetically.*) But what the hell! Don't let me be a wet blanket, making fool speeches about myself. Set 'em up again, Rocky. Here. (*He pulls a big roll from his pocket and peels off a ten-dollar bill. The faces of all brighten.*) Keep the balls coming until this is killed. Then ask for more.

ROCKY Jees, a roll dat'd choke a hippopotamus! Fill up, youse guys.

They all pour out drinks.

George Orwell

George Orwell was said to have had a good head for alcohol, an indispensable characteristic for BBC types in the halcyon days when pubs acted as a sort of employment exchange, before the grey men partial to mineral water took over. Certainly, he needed a good head to cope with characters such as Dylan Thomas, whom he took on as a poetry reader, and drank with after the broadcasts at various pubs including one known as the Whores' Lament after the American military had left London for France.

It is doubtful if Orwell was ever what could be described as a pubby man. He was probably happier in restaurants with friends such as Malcolm Muggeridge (in his pre-canonization days), Anthony Powell and Julian Symons. He did, however, enjoy dragging intellectual colleagues to pubs, and mocking them when they failed to respond with appropriate enthusiasm.

He approved of pubs and beer, perhaps on intellectual grounds, as evidence of the solid, genuine values of working-class life as compared with those of the effete bourgeois. He was probably a touch romantic in his views of the importance of the pub, lamenting in the 1940s about the move from the communal amusement of pub life to the 'mechanical' pleasures of the cinema and radio. It is interesting to speculate on what he would have made of the entertainment available in pubs in the latter stages of the twentieth century.

And it is clear that working-class stalwarts were thin on the ground in the pubs of Fitzrovia and Soho used by Orwell, where shouted orders for drinks had to compete with enthusiastic descriptions of planned plays, novels and poems – many of which ended there, drifting away in clouds of tobacco smoke and alcohol fumes.

He was utterly fascinated by working-class culture, in a way only an Old Etonian could be. It was, for him, truly new. He identified with it, as far as he was able, as the extract from *The Moon Under Water* illustrates. Some may think the reference to beer served in strawberry-coloured china jugs strikes a false note, as today's drinkers prefer plain glass and connoisseurs of beer insist that thin glasses without handles are the only possible ones to use. Personally, I prefer jugs as they are less likely to slip from the hand in crowded pubs and I would rather use a china jug than the pewter mugs certain drinking men insist on hanging in the pub as a symbol of their fidelity to the establishment.

The Moon under Water

My favourite public house, the Moon under Water, is only two minutes from a bus stop, but it is on a side-street, and drunks and rowdies never seem to find their way there, even on Saturday nights.

Its clientele, though fairly large, consists mostly of 'regulars' who occupy the same chair every evening and go there for conversation as much as for the beer.

If you are asked why you favour a particular public house, it would seem natural to put the beer first, but the thing that most appeals to me about the Moon under Water is what people call its 'atmosphere'.

To begin with, its whole architecture and fittings are uncompromisingly Victorian. It has no glass-topped tables or other modern miseries, and, on the other hand, no sham roof-beams, inglenooks or plastic panels masquerading as oak. The grained woodwork, the ornamental mirrors behind the bar, the cast-iron fire-places, the florid ceiling stained dark yellow by tobacco-smoke, the stuffed bull's head over the mantlepiece – everything has the solid comfortable ugliness of the nineteenth century.

In winter there is generally a good fire burning in at least two of the bars, and the Victorian lay-out of the place gives one plenty of elbow-room. There is a public bar, a saloon bar, a ladies' bar, a bottle-and-jug for those who are too bashful to buy their supper beer publicly, and upstairs, a dining-room.

Games are only played in the public, so that in the other bars you can walk about without constantly ducking to avoid flying darts.

In the Moon under Water it is always quiet enough to talk. The house possesses neither a radio nor a piano, and even on Christmas Eve and such occasions the singing that happens is of a decorous kind.

The barmaids know most of their customers by name, and take a personal interest in everyone. They are all middle-aged women – two of them have their hair dyed in quite surprising shades – and they call everyone 'dear' irrespective of age or sex. ('Dear', not 'Ducky'; pubs where the barmaid calls you 'Ducky' always have a disagreeable raffish atmosphere.)

Unlike most pubs, the Moon under Water sells tobacco as well as cigarettes, and it also sells aspirins and stamps, and is obliging about letting you use the telephone.

You cannot get dinner at the Moon under Water, but there is always the snack counter where you can get liver-sausage sandwiches, mussels (a speciality of the house), cheese, pickles and those large biscuits with caraway seeds in them which only seem to exist in public houses.

Upstairs, six days a week, you can get a good, solid lunch – for example, a cut off the joint, two vegetables and boiled jam roll – for about three shillings.

The special pleasure of this lunch is that you can have draught stout with it. I doubt whether as many as ten per cent of London pubs serve draught stout, but the Moon under Water is one of them. It is a soft, creamy sort of stout, and it goes better in a pewter pot.

They are particular about their drinking vessels at the Moon under Water and never, for example, make the mistake of serving a pint of beer in a handleless glass. Apart from glass and pewter mugs, they have some of those pleasant strawberry-pink china ones which are now seldom seen in London. China mugs went out about thirty years ago, because most people like their drink to be transparent, but in my opinion beer tastes better out of china.

The great surprise of the Moon under Water is its garden. You go through a narrow passage leading out of the saloon, and find yourself in a fairly large garden with plane trees under which there are little green tables with iron chairs round them. Up at one end of the garden there are swings and a chute for the children.

On summer evenings there are family parties, and you sit under the plane trees having beer or draught cider to the tune of delighted squeals from children going down the chute. The prams with the younger children are parked near the gate.

Many as are the virtues of the Moon under Water I think that the garden is its best feature, because it allows whole families to go there instead of Mum having to stay at home and mind the baby while Dad goes out alone.

And though, strictly speaking, they are only allowed in the garden, the children tend to seep into the pub and even to fetch drinks for their parents. This, I believe, is against the law, but it is a law that deserves to be broken, for it is the puritanical nonsense of excluding children – and therefore to some extent, women – from pubs that has turned these places into mere boozing-shops instead of the family gathering-places that they ought to be.

The Moon under Water is my ideal of what a pub should be – at any rate, in the London area. (The qualities one expects of a country pub are slightly different.)

But now is the time to reveal something which the discerning and disillusioned reader will probably have guessed already.

George
Orwell
and
Dylan Thomas

That is to say, there may well be a pub of that name, but I don't know of it, nor do I know any pub with just that combination of qualities.

I know pubs where the beer is good but you can't get meals, others where you can get meals but which are noisy and crowded, and others which are quiet but where the beer is generally sour. As for gardens, offhand I can only think of three London pubs that possess them.

But, to be fair, I do know of a few pubs that almost come up to the Moon under Water. I have mentioned above ten qualities that the perfect pub should have, and I know one pub that has eight of them. Even there, however, there is no draught stout and no china mugs.

And if anyone knows of a pub that has draught stout, open fires, cheap meals, a garden, motherly barmaids and no radio, I should be glad to hear of it, even though its name were something as prosaic as the Red Lion or the Railway Arms.

Dylan Thomas

Dylan Thomas was the most influential poet of his generation, the embodiment of Welshness in himself and in his language. Drinking seems to have been a way of life for him, an unwavering road from the pubs of Swansea to the bars, clubs and pubs of Fitzrovia where he spent so much of his time in talk and drinking. In company with others, he roared the nights away on a flood of beer (his favourite drink) and adjectives, often sleeping it off in the room of some tender-hearted girl. Although a metropolitan drinker, he once claimed to have downed forty pints in a memorable session on holiday in Cornwall.

Thomas was a star turn in any pub, an irresistibly eloquent and funny teller of Welsh tall tales – it is said he left Wales with a pronounced English accent and managed to develop a Welsh lilt while in London.

A favourite game during his binges was Cats and Dogs which involved him running around on all fours, taking a bite out of any leg to which he took a fancy. Not surprisingly, not everyone found this game amusing, but his high-octane charm was usually enough to disarm criticism. Women adored him, often older, well-off women such as Dame Edith Sitwell and Margaret Taylor, wife of A J P Taylor. Dylan adored them in turn, finding them a useful source of funds – he was a lifelong, unrepentant scrounger.

Despite his heavy drinking, some friends argued that Thomas was not an alcoholic. In fact, it was said he had a low tolerance for alcohol and thus needed little drink to become drunk. On the other hand, his own accounts of his drinking habits tell of copious amounts of booze, but it should be remembered he was notorious for exaggeration.

All the evidence from Wales, London and America shows a wild, exuberant spirit, intoxicated on drink, or words or dreams, a poet living out a legend.

His novel *Adventures in the Skin Trade* – part fiction, part autobiography – perfectly captures the hazy, wandering, rambling, sometimes nightmarish nature of a night on the town.

Adventures in the Skin Trade

'Don't you call me morbid, George Ring … I remember once I drank forty-nine Guinnesses straight off and I came home on top of a bus. There's nothing morbid about a man who can do that. Right on top of the bus, too, not just in the upper deck.'

'I think forty-nine Guinnesses is piggish,' said George Ring.

'It was raining,' Mr Allingham said, 'and I never get truculent. I may sing and I may dance but I never get nasty.'

The Cheerioh was a bad blaze, an old hole light. In the dark, open a cupboard full of cast-off clothes moving in a wind from nowhere, the smell of mothballs and damp furs, and find a lamp lit, candles burning, a gramophone playing …

The men and women drinking and dancing looked like the older brothers and sisters of the drinkers and dancers in the club round the corner, but no one was black. There deep green faces, dipped in a sea dye, with painted cockles for mouths and lichenous hair, sealed on the cheeks; red and purple, slate-grey, tide-marked, rat-brown and stickily whitewashed, with violet-inked eyes or lips the colour of Stilton; pink chopped, pink lidded, pink as the belly of a newborn monkey, nicotine yellow with mustard flecked eyes, rust scraping through the bleach, black hairs axle-greased down among the peroxide; squashed fly stubbles, saltcellarded necks thick with pepper powder; carrot heads, yolk-heads, black-heads, heads bald as sweet-breads.

'All white people here,' Samuel said.

'The salt of the earth,' Mr Allingham said, 'the foul salt of the earth. Drunk as a pig. Ever seen a pig drunk? Ever seen a monkey dancing like a man? Look at that king of the animals.'

Emile Zola

Among the many compliments showered on Emile Zola's mighty novel of the destructive effect of drunkenness, *L'Assommoir*, perhaps the most telling was that it was adopted by the temperance movement as a text against drink.

Although it was probably not what the author would have expected or intended, the temperance movement made a good choice, as Zola, a visionary and social reformer, paints a frightening picture of the potential effects of alcohol. In the novel Zola describes the real world of the poor of Paris of his day, where absinthe and brandy at one franc a litre offered an escape route from a life of unmitigated misery.

Although Zola knew something of that world from his early, penurious days in Paris, he relied on thorough research – as in all his works – to provide the bedrock, the basis on which his powerful imagination would work. He observed the dozens of dingy bars in the slums – from which the title of the book is taken – and studied patients in hospital suffering from alcoholism.

Zola himself, however, was a gourmet, a man of taste fond of wining and dining his friends. Daudet recalled the first meeting of the celebrated dinners of the five, Diners les Cinq, when Zola, Flaubert, Goncourt, Turgenev and himself met to eat, drink and talk. He remembered the dishes chosen: *canards rouennais a l'estouffade* for Flaubert; caviar for Turgenev; sea-urchins and shell-fish for Zola. Flaubert and Zola set to in shirtsleeves and Daudet reveals 'we used to sit down at seven o'clock and had not finished till 2 in the morning'. Many varied wines were drunk on these occasions and the talk was likely to descend from high art to earthier subjects as the night wore on.

Another literary-social group gathered around Zola in the 1880s, younger writers who shared Zola's views on realism. The first dinner was organized by Maupassant and a spoof menu published which promised such delights as: *Potage purée Bovary*, *Parfait Naturaliste*, *Vin de Coupeau* and *Liqueur de L'Assommoir*. The group often met at Medan, Zola's country home outside Paris, for food, drink and lighthearted conversation. Zola was a good host – 'he has a feeling and a taste for hospitality' said Daudet.

Goncourt recorded in his diary one of the regular dinners held at Medan in the 1880s: 'A marvellous dinner. Domestic in white tie. Mme Zola low-cut, bare-bosomed. Seven glasses, with the wines specified ... In this comedy of elegance, Zola playing the genial host.'

All this is a far cry from the sordid, fetid, brutal world of *L'Assommoir* in which the characters seem helpless to avoid or escape their fate.

L'Assommoir

The place was flaring, the gas alight, white flames like suns, the jars and bottles illuminating the walls with their coloured glass. She stood there an instant leaning forward, with her face against the glass, between two bottles in the window, peering at Coupeau, who was sitting with his friends at the other end of the place, at a little zinc-topped table, all vague and misty in the smoke of their pipes ... The rain dripped in her neck; she moved away and went on to the outer boulevard, turning it over in her mind, not venturing to go in ... Twice she went back and stood outside the window, putting her face against the glass again, vexed to see those infernal drunkards in out of the rain, chatting and drinking. The light of the bar was reflected in the puddles of the pavements, where the rain pattered and bubbled. She stepped back and splashed into it whenever the door opened and shut, creaking on its rusty hinges. After all she was merely coming after her husband; and she had a right to for he had promised to take her to the circus that evening. Well, here goes! she was not going to melt out there on the pavement, like a cake of soap.

... Old fat Colombe, reaching out his huge arms, the terror of the establishment, calmly served out drinks. It was very hot, the smoke of pipes went up in the blinding glitter of gaslight, spreading like a cloud of dust, and covering the drinkers with a slowly thickening steam; and out of this cloud there came a deafening, confused hubbub of cracked voices and the clink of glasses, oaths and blows of the fist, like detonations. Gervaise made a wry face, for a sight like that is not a very entertaining one for a woman, especially when she is not used to it; she choked, her eyes burnt, her head swam in the alcoholic smell exhaled by the whole place.

… 'I say, mealy-mouth!' cried Coupeau, 'don't make faces. Wet blankets may go to Jericho! What'll you have to drink?'

'Nothing, certainly,' replied the laundress, 'I haven't had dinner.'

'All the more reason; a drop of something will keep you up.'

But as she still kept a glum visage, Mes-Bottes once more came forward politely.

'The lady surely likes liqueurs,' he murmured.

'I like men who don't get drunk,' she answered surlily. 'Yes, I like people to bring back their pay and keep their word when they have made a promise.'

'Ah! that's what upsets you!' said the tinsmith, still laughing. 'You want your share. Well, you blockhead, why don't you have a drink? You'd better have it, it's all profit.'

She looked straight in his face, very seriously, wrinkling her forehead till a black furrow came out all across. And she answered slowly:

'So be it, you are right, it's a good idea. We'll drink the cash together.'

Bibi-la-Grillade went to get her a glass of anisette. She pulled up her chair to the table. As she sipped her anisette she remembered all at once how she had had a prune with Coupeau, long ago, there near the door, when he was courting her. At that time she left the brandy sauce. And now here she was drinking liqueurs again. Oh! she knew herself now, she had not a halfpennyworth of will. She only wanted a good kick behind to send her headlong into the drink.

… 'You'll have another madame?'

No, she had had enough. Still, she hesitated. The anisette was not quite the thing. She would rather have had something a little sharper, to settle her stomach. And she glanced sideways at the drinking machine behind her. The blessed object, round as a publican's belly, with its nose that trailed and twisted, sent a shiver through her, half fear, half desire. It might have been the metallic intestines of some sorceress, distilling, drop by drop, the fire that burnt within her. It was a poisonous thing, a thing that should have been hidden away in a cellar, so shameless and abominable was it! But, all the same, she was drawn to the thing, would fain have sniffed at its odour, tasted its bestiality, even if her tongue had burnt and peeled off like an orange.

Remorse and Recovery

We continued drinking like horses, as the vulgar phrase is, and singing till many of us were very drunk, and then we went to dancing and pulling of wigs, caps, and hats; and thus we continued in this frantic manner, behaving more like mad people than they that profess the name of Christians. Whether this is consistent to the wise saying of Solomon, let any one judge; 'Wine is a mocker, strong drink is raging, and he that is deceived thereby is not wise.'

Thomas Turner

K AMIS	*Lucky Jim*
R BURNS	Letter to Mrs Robert Riddell
LORD BYRON	*Don Juan*
G CHAUCER	*The Canterbury Tales*
C DICKENS	*Martin Chuzzlewit*
C LAMB	Letter to Dr J V Asbury
M LOWRY	*Under the Volcano*
S PEPYS	*Diary*

Kingsley Amis

Whatever Kingsley Amis's merits as a writer – and there are those who claim he is easily the greatest English novelist of the last quarter of the twentieth century – he was an outstanding and accomplished drinker.

Unlike many other writers – or public figures in general – he made no secret of his fondness for drink and its central role in his life. He once wrote a slim volume on the subject – curiously, rather slimmer than one might have expected given his experience – which is a kind of plain man's guide to drinking. Its principal interest is that it shows how even a very good, witty writer can produce the occasional dud, but it has the odd helpful, if esoteric advice on such matters as coping with a hangover: one suggestion is vigorous sexual intercourse.

Amis consumed large quantities all his life, without regrets or excuses. He was an unrepentant heavy drinker but by no means an alcoholic, a term which he regarded as abusive rather than diagnostic. He believed in the definition, supplied by a doctor, that 'an alcoholic is a man who drinks more than his doctor'.

During a lifetime of drinking at regular intervals throughout the day, he worked as a professional writer, producing novels, poetry, newspaper and magazine articles by the hundred, which suggests his way of life hardly hindered his work. Drink was a constant theme in his life. There were well-remembered binges in the army and overwhelming hospitality in the United States, where he was teaching – in Nashville he reckoned he had had a hangover every day of his stay.

Drink had a high priority in his life. When his second wife insisted he gave up drinking as a condition of their marriage, he chose to continue drinking.

In later life, as described by Eric Jacobs in his frank but friendly biography, the drinking day began with a large Macallan malt and water, the first of two or three before lunch in his local pub or at his club, the Garrick. Lunch followed at two o'clock, during which there was wine followed by a Venise de Beaume or Grand Marnier. Then home and a nap, after which more work until about seven o'clock and more Macallan and Evian water until supper, at which there was usually beer. During the rest of the evening there would be more splashes of Macallan and a tot as a nightcap before retiring.

Lucky Jim

The night of the Party

It wasn't as nice in the bathroom as it had been in the bedroom. Though it was a cool night for early summer, he found he felt hot and was sweating. He stood for some time in front of the wash-basin, trying to discover more about how he felt. His body seemed swollen below the chest and uneven in density. The stuff coming from the light seemed less like light than a very thin but cloudy phosphorescent gas; it gave a creamy hum. He turned on the cold tap and bent over the basin. When he did this, he had to correct an impulse to go on leaning forward until his head lay between the taps. He wetted his face, took a bakelite mug from the glass shelf above the basin, and drank a very great deal of water, which momentarily refreshed him, though it had some other effect as well which he couldn't at once identify. He cleaned his teeth with a lot of toothpaste, wetted his face again, refilled the mug, and ate some more toothpaste.

He stood brooding by his bed. His face was heavy, as if little bags of sand had been painlessly sewn into various parts of it, dragging the features away from the bones, if he still had bones in his face. Suddenly feeling worse, he heaved a shuddering sigh. Someone seemed to have leapt nimbly up behind him and encased him in a kind of diving-suit made of invisible cotton-wool. He gave a quiet groan; he didn't want to feel any worse than this.

He began getting into bed. His four surviving cigarettes – had he really smoked twelve that evening? – lay in their packet on a polished table at the bed-head, accompanied by matches, the bakelite mug of water, and an ashtray from the mantelpiece. A temporary inability to raise his second foot on to the bed let him know what had been the secondary effect of drinking all that water: it had made him drunk. This became a primary effect when he lay in bed. On the fluttering mantelpiece was a small china effigy, the representation, in a squatting position, of a well-known Oriental religious figure. Had Welch put it there as a silent sermon to him on the merits of the contemplative life? If so, the message had come too late. He reached up and turned off the light by the hanging switch above his head. The room began to rise upwards from the right-hand bottom corner of the bed, and yet seemed to keep in the same position. He threw back the covers and sat on the edge of the bed, his legs hanging. The room composed itself to rest. After a few moments he swung his legs back and lay down. The room lifted. He put his feet to the floor. The room stayed still. He put his legs on the bed but didn't lie down. The room moved. He sat on the edge of the bed. Nothing. He put one leg up on the bed. Something. In fact a great deal. He was evidently in a highly critical condition. Swearing hoarsely, he heaped up the pillows, half-lay, half-sat against them, and dangled his legs half-over the edge of the bed. In this position he was able to lower himself gingerly into sleep.

The Morning After

Dixon was alive again. Consciousness was upon him before he could get out of the way; not for him the slow, gracious wandering from the halls of sleep, but a summary, forcible ejection. He lay sprawled, too wicked to move, spewed up like a broken spider-crab on the tarry shingle of the morning. The light did him harm, but not as much as looking at things did; he resolved, having done it once, never to move his eye-balls again. A dusty thudding in his head made the scene before him beat like a pulse. His mouth had been used as a latrine by some small creature of the night, and then as its mausoleum. During the night, too, he'd somehow been on a cross-country run and then been expertly beaten up by the secret police. He felt bad.

Robert Burns

The personality of Robert Burns is engaging and familiar, even to those who have never read much of his poetry. From the evidence of his poetry and of his life he had two passions – women and drink – and it is difficult to say which was the more powerful.

People born outside Scotland cannot fully understand the feelings Scots have about a man who is not only a national poet but a national hero. Despite the efforts of some well-meaning Scots folk to present him as a man of moderation, he remains an icon for the people, a loveable rogue, a randy lad, a spirited hell-raiser, drunk on whisky and high emotions. Proud and sober Scots find it hard to accept a national treasure on these terms and are often driven to explain his excesses – he was a moderate drinker or had no head for drink, he has been much maligned, and so on. But the evidence, gentlemen, the evidence!

It sometimes seems that many drunken Scotsmen, at a certain point in their revelries, become convinced they are reincarnations of the national bard. The solitary drunk winding his way home in the dark of night, after drinking to soften disappointment in love or sport or both, with a few faltering words of Burns on his lips is an example of the type. So, too, is the dedicated follower who is able to recite at interminable length what seems to be every verse of the very many the great man penned. On the whole, those not of Scottish origin can only look on with awe and stupefaction as the declamation winds on, loud, vigorous and impenetrable.

What is perfectly clear, however, is the emphasis given to drink in his poetry. Indeed, it is hard to think of any other poet so dedicated to praise of alcohol. There are exhortations everywhere, impassioned pleas, shouts of praise. For example:

> But let the kirk-folk ring their bells!
> Let's sing about our noble sel's:
> We'll cry nae jads frae heathen hills
> To help or roose us,
> But browster wives an' whisky stills –
> They are the Muses!

(jads = jades, roose = arouse, browster wives = ale wives)

Letter to Mrs Robert Riddell

Madam,

I dare say that this is the first epistle you ever received from this nether world. I write you from the regions of Hell, amid the horrors of the damn'd. The time and manner of my leaving your earth I do not exactly know, as I took my departure in the heat of a fever of intoxication, contracted at your too Hospitable mansion; but, on my arrival here, I was fairly tried, and sentenced to endure the purgatorial tortures of this infernal confine for the space of ninety-nine years, eleven months and twenty-nine days, and all on account of the impropriety of my conduct yesternight under your roof. Here am I, laid on a bed of pitiless furze, with my aching head reclined on a pillow of ever-piercing thorn, while an infernal tormentor, wrinkled, and old, and crule, his name I think is *Recollection*, with a whip of scorpions, forbids peace or rest to approach me, and keeps anguish eternally awake. Still, Madam, if I could in any measure be reinstated in the good opinion of the fair circle whom my conduct last night so much injured, I think it would be an alleviation to my torments. For this reason I trouble you with this letter. To the men of the company I will make no apology. – Your husband, who insisted on my drinking more than I chose, has no right to blame me; and the other gentlemen were partakers of my guilt. But to you, Madam, I have much to apologize. Your good opinion I valued as one of the greatest acquisitions I had made on earth, and I was truly a beast to forfeit it. There was a Miss I— too, a woman of fine sense, gentle and unassuming manners – do make, on my part, a miserable damn'd wretch's best apology to her. A Mrs G—, a charming woman, did me the honour to be prejudiced in my favour; this makes me hope that I have not outraged her beyond all forgiveness. – To all the other ladies please present my humblest contrition for my conduct, and my petition for their gracious pardon. O all ye powers of decency and decorum! whisper to them that my errors, though great, were involuntary – that an intoxicated man is the vilest of beasts – that it was not in my nature to be brutal to any one – that to be rude to a woman, when in my senses, was impossible with me – but – Regret! Remorse! Shame! ye three hellbounds that ever dog my steps and bay at my heels, spare me!

Forgive the offences, and pity the perdition of, Madam,

Your humble Slave,
(Robt. Burns)

*

Lord Byron

Although described as 'mad, bad and dangerous to know', Lord Byron drank and whored in the way expected of a gentleman of his age. He was handsome, brilliant, popular and rich enough to indulge his appetites to the full; which, of course, he immediately set about doing.

There was a well-stocked cellar at the family estate, Newstead. An inventory of a proposed sale of the property in 1815 showed the cellar had '20 dozen quart bottles of port, 1 doz more which had been 14yrs in bott. 4 doz particularly fine Bucellas and 34 of white and 6 of red Hermitage plus 24 of very curious old Madeira.' (Bucellas is a golden Portuguese wine, popular at the time but seldom seen today outside Portugal.)

He described festivities at Newstead:

> where I had got a famous cellar, and Monks' dresses from a masquerade warehouse. We were a company of some seven or eight, with an occasional neighbour or so for visitors, and used to sit up late in our friars' dresses, drinking burgundy, claret, champagne and whatnot, out of the skull-cup, and all sorts of glasses, and buffooning all round the house.

On another occasion he was drinking with friends

> at the Cocoa Tree, from six till four, yea, unto five in the matin. We clareted and champagned till two – then supped, and finished with a kind of regency punch composed of madeira, brandy and green tea, no real water being admitted therein. That was a night for you! Without once quitting the table … I have also, more or less, been breaking a few of the favourite commandments.

Not surprisingly, his marriage was a disastrous and short-lived affair. His wife, Annabella, accused him of flinging soda-water bottles at the ceiling of the room beneath her bedroom where she was in labour, so they exploded under the bed in which she was lying.

Hock and soda, the modern spritzer, was a favourite drink, light to digest after a night's debauchery, although gin and water was said to be his drink of choice when writing poetry. At table he preferred fine

Lord Byron

claret: 'I hate anonymous wine,' he said. A generous host, he encouraged his guests to make 'claret vats' of themselves.

Gin loomed large on his travels in Europe. In Italy he enjoyed gin punch with lemons, *limonnata serale*, in the evening. Gin punch for picnics was usual, and guests enjoyed the 'glorious gin swizzle' made up from two-gallon jars.

In Venice there were pleasures to rival those of drinking, as Byron remarked:

> Fiddling, feasting, dancing, drinking, masking
> And other things which may be had for asking.

Supplies taken to Greece, where Byron travelled to aid the cause of Greek independence, included some prosaic bottles of Burton ale. These were augmented by the local wine but Byron's servant, Fletcher, complained that it tasted more of turpentine than grapes – a criticism often made of Greek wine in modern times.

It was while in Greece that Byron contracted a fever and died young, at the age of 36, thus ensuring his lasting fame as a romantic hero.

Don Juan

Hock and Soda Water

Few things surpass old wine; and they may preach
Who please – the more because they preach in vain.
Let us have wine and woman, mirth and laughter,
Sermons and soda water the day after.

Man being reasonable must get drunk;
The best of life is but intoxication.
Glory, the grape, love, gold, in these are sunk
The hopes of all men and every nation;
Without their sap, how branchless were the trunk
Of life's strange tree, so fruitful on occasion.
But to return. Get very drunk, and when
You wake with headache, you shall see what then.

Ring for your valet, bid him quickly bring
Some hock and soda water. Then you'll know

A pleasure worthy Xerxes, the great king;
For not the blest sherbet, sublimed with snow,
Nor the first sparkle of the desert spring,
Nor Burgundy in all its sunset glow,
After long travel, ennui, love, or slaughter,
Vie with that draught of hock and soda water.

Reeling Drunk

I would to heaven that I were so much clay,
As I am blood, bone, marrow, passion, feeling –
Because at least the past were pass'd away –
And for the future – (but I write this reeling
Having got drunk exceedingly to-day,
So that I seem to stand upon the ceiling)
I say – the future is a serious matter –
And so – for God's sake – hock and soda water!

Geoffrey Chaucer

Geoffrey Chaucer is widely known as England's first great writer, the Father of English Poetry and other venerable titles. It is less well known that he had a deep and expert knowledge of the wine trade because both his father and grandfather were in the wine business. Chaucer himself, among other duties such as diplomat and administrator, worked as a kind of tax collector when in charge of customs on wine in the Port of London. His allowance of a pitcher of wine a day in the service of Edward III became, under Richard II, an annual tun of 954 litres.

Chaucer was a courtier and highly educated but his work conveys a picture of a world which is vulgar, outspoken, full flavoured and gamey. He was clearly a man of the world, completely at home with the common people, as can be seen in the descriptions of drunken exploits in the 'Reeves' Tale'; the ripe vulgarity of the 'Miller's Tale' and the lusty pragmatism of the Wife of Bath, who admitted cheerfully, in Alexander Pope's translation:

Whenever I take wine I have to think
Of Venus, for as cold engenders hail
A lecherous mouth begets a lecherous tail.
A woman in her cups has no defence,
As lechers know from long experience.

In the Middle Ages four humours or states were identified: choleric, sanguine, phlegmatic and melancholic. Doctors prescribed diets according to the humours of their patients: the sanguine man, for example, was advised to forgo meat in favour of fish.

The same humours emerged in drink – thus the choleric was said to be lion-drunk; the sanguine ape-drunk; the phlegmatic mutton-drunk; and the melancholic swine-drunk (these characteristics are familiar among the drinking classes of today).

Chaucer also shows that little has changed not only in terms of the appetite for drink but in the ingenuity of those determined to obtain it illegally. A couple of lines in *The Canterbury Tales* reveal how little human nature changes from century to century:

I know that ye dronken han wyn ape,
And that is when men pleyeth with a straw!

(You'd think he had been drinking monkey-wine,
And that's when one goes playing with a straw!)

In the early years of this century, workers were sometimes found comatose after gorging on wine stolen from wine warehouses. Such people were said to have been 'sucking the monkey', in dockside slang. The term meant drilling a tiny hole in the side of a cask of wine and sucking out the liquid through a straw. The pipette used for drawing out wine samples was sometimes called a thief tube or monkey-pump. Xenophon, writing in the fifth century BC, described this method used by workers pilfering from the wine-jars of Armenia. *Plus ça change* …

The Canterbury Tales

The Manciple's Prologue

'Wake up, you Cook!' he said. 'God give you sorrow,
What's up with you to sleep this sunny morrow?

Have you had fleas all night, or else got drunk,
Or spent the night in toiling with a punk,
And haven't got the strength to raise your head?'
The Cook was drunk, pale-drunk, no touch of red,
And answered from a stupor, 'Bless my soul!
I feel all heavy, haven't got control;
I'd rather sleep,' he said, 'I don't know why,
Than drink a gallon of wine, the best you buy
In all Cheapside.' The Manciple said, 'Well,
If I can make things easier for a spell
For you, and not offend the company,
And if the Host extends his courtesy
To let me, I'll excuse you from your tale.
'Upon my word, your face is pretty pale,
Your eyes are somewhat dazed, I can't help thinking,
As for your breath, I'm bound to say it's stinking,
Which shows you indisposed for such a matter,
Blunt words are best, I never was one to flatter.
'Look at him yawning there, the drunken sot!
You'd think he meant to swallow us on the spot.
Keep your mouth shut, man! mercy, what a socket!
The devil of Hell's own hoof would hardly block it;
Your cursed breath may well infect us all.
You stinking swine, fie, how you gape and sprawl!
(Look out, take care, sir, he's a powerful man)
I'd like to see a punch-ball hit his pan!
He's about ripe for trouble in that line;
You'd think he had been drinking monkey-wine,
And that's when one goes playing with a straw!'
This speech annoyed the Cook who, turning raw,
Craned at the Manciple with so much force
For want of speech, he tumbled off his horse
And there he lay for all the care they took;
Fine cavalry performance for a cook!
Pity he couldn't have held on by his ladle.
They got him back at last into the cradle
After a deal of shoving to and fro
To lift him up, it was a sorry show;
Poor, pallid soul, unwielder than most!
But to the Manciple at last our Host

Turned and remarked, 'Drink is in domination
Over the fellow; by my soul's salvation
I think he'd only tell a lousy tale,
Whether it's wine or maybe new-brewed ale
That's in him, he is talking through his nose;
Like someone with a cold, one would suppose,
Snuffling like that. I think he's going to spew,
It's just about as much as he can do
To keep his horse from falling in the ditch
And if his horse should fall, he'll follow, which
Gives us as much as we can do to strain
And lift his drunken body up again.'

Charles Dickens

Readers of Dickens need no convincing that nobody enjoyed and understood pubs more than the author, and no other writer created such an entertaining and convincing collection of drinkers. These immortal inebriates reel through the pages of his work: Sarah Gamp, infinitely dignified, even when slightly 'indisposed'; that fierce drinker of rum, Mr Quilp; the drunken but noble Sydney Carton. Sam Weller, according to his father, was able to absorb much liquid. His father told him he 'would ha' made an uncommon fine oyster, Sammy, if you'd been born in that station o' life'. There is the gentleman of the old school in *Barnaby Rudge* who 'could eat more solid food, drink more strong wine, go to bed every night more drunk and get up every morning more sober, than any man in the country'.

Dickens himself was not a heavy drinker, although he had done his share of carousing in youth, as is perhaps evident in his description of the condition of David Copperfield during a lively celebration. David recalls his friend, Steerforth, asking him, ' "Are you all right, Copperfield, are you not?" and I told him "Neverberrer".' And later, when the celebrations had ended and he was in bed: 'I begin to parch, and feel as if my outer covering of skin were a hard board; my tongue the bottom of an empty kettle, furred with long service, and burning up over a slow fire; the palms of my hands, hot plates of metal which no ice could cool.'

Charles Dickens
with great expectations

In later life Dickens drank sherry and seltzer for lunch and eggs beaten in sherry to fortify him during his public readings; he also enjoyed champagne. His cellar at Gads Hill was that of a man of substance. The contents were revealed in a catalogue of the sale in August 1870: '4 dozen cyder; 12 dozen sherry, dry golden sherry; 18 bottles sherry solera; 1 dozen sherry, old dry pale; 1 dozen amontillado; 13 magnums of gold sherry; 4 dozen rare old madeira; 5 dozen port, 22yrs in bottle; 18 magnums port, vintage 1851; 5 dozen port vintage 1851; 16 dozen medoc; 3 dozen margaux; 5doz leoville; 13botts chateau d'issan 1858; 16botts clos vougeot; 16botts Volnay; 17doz champagne Bouzy; 8doz dry champagne; 18doz old pale brandy from courvoisier; 17doz very fine old Highland whisky – plus gin, sauterne, Australian wine, apple wine'. A cellar designed to meet all eventualities, it must be said.

The information about the Gads Hill cellar comes from another Dickens, Cedric, the writer's great-grandson, who has collected much interesting information about drink and his illustrious ancestor. Brandy, he informs us, is mentioned forty-four times in *The Pickwick Papers*. Cedric also offers a personal contribution in one of his books, on how to avoid jet lag. The advice is simple: drink one bottle of champagne before the flight and a quarter of a bottle on the hour every hour without food. If the recipe works, excellent, if it fails, it is, at least, enjoyable.

Martin Chuzzlewit

She was a fat old woman, this Mrs. Gamp, with a husky voice and a moist eye, which she had a remarkable power of turning up, and only showing the white of it. Having very little neck, it cost her some trouble to look over herself, if one may say so, at those to whom she talked. She wore a very rusty black gown, rather the worse for snuff, and a shawl and bonnet to correspond. In these dilapidated articles of dress she had, on principle, arrayed herself, time out of mind, on such occasions as the present; for this at once expressed a decent amount of veneration for the deceased, and invited the next of kin to present her with a fresher suit of weeds; an appeal so frequently successful, that the very fetch and ghost of Mrs. Gamp, bonnet and all, might be seen hanging up, any hour of the day, in at least a dozen of the second-hand shops about Holborn. The face of Mrs. Gamp – the nose in particular – was somewhat red and swollen, and it was difficult to enjoy her society without becoming conscious of a smell of spirits. Like most persons who have attained to great eminence in their profession, she took to hers very kindly; insomuch, that setting aside her natural predilections as a woman, she went to a lying-in or a laying-out with equal zest and relish.

'Ah!' repeated Mrs. Gamp; for it was always a safe sentiment in case of mourning. 'Ah dear! When Gamp was summoned to his long home, and I see him a lying in Guy's Hospital with a penny-piece on each eye, and his wooden leg under his left arm, I thought I should have fainted away. But I bore up.'

If certain whispers current in the Kingsgate Street circles had any truth in them, she had indeed borne up surprisingly; and had exerted such uncommon fortitude, as to dispose of Mr. Gamp's remains for the benefit of science. But it should be added, in fairness, that his had happened twenty years before; and that Mr and Mrs. Gamp had long been separated, on the ground of incompatibility of temper in their drink.

'You have become indifferent since then, I suppose?' said Mr. Pecksniff. 'Use is second nature, Mrs. Gamp.'

'You may well say second nater, sir,' returned that lady. 'One's first ways is to find sich things a trial for the feelings, and so is one's lasting custom. If it wasn't for the nerve a little sip of liquor give me (I never was able to do more than taste it), I never could go through with what I sometimes has to do. "Mrs. Harris," I says, at the very last case as ever I acted in, which it was but a young person, "Mrs. Harris," I says, "leave the bottle on the chimley-piece, and don't ask me to take none, but let me put my lips to it when I am so dispoged, and I will do what I'm engaged to do, according to the best of my ability." "Mrs. Gamp," she says, in answer, "if ever there was a sober creetur to be got at eighteen pence a day for working people, and three and six for gentlefolks – night watching," ' said Mrs. Gamp, with emphasis, ' "being an extra charge – you are that inwallable person." "Mrs. Harris," I says to her, "don't name the charge, for if I could afford to lay all my feller creeturs out for nothink, I would gladly do it sich is the love I bears 'em. But what I always says to them as has the management of matters, Mrs. Harris;" ' here she kept her eye on Mr Pecksniff: ' "be they gents or be they ladies, is, don't ask me

> whether I won't take none, or whether I will, but leave the bottle on the chimley-piece, and let me put my lips to it when I am so dispoged." '

Charles Lamb

Charles Lamb was an unusual drinker in one important respect: he never seems to have annoyed or alienated anyone when in his cups, a condition that he was in fairly frequently. He confessed that he was often 'half tipsy' on gin-and-water, a common and cheap drink of the period.

His friends included De Quincey, Coleridge, Keats, Hazlitt, Wordsworth and just about everybody in early nineteenth-century literary London. They all appear to have loved his company, especially when he was drinking, even though they knew that Lamb's brilliant, spirited talk could be stilled by sudden sleep. De Quincey gave a memorable description of Lamb nodding off:

> Over Lamb … there passed regularly, after taking wine, a brief eclipse of sleep. It descended upon him as a shadow. In a gross person, laden with superfluous flesh, this would have been disagreeable; but in Lamb, thin to meagreness, spare and wiry as an Arab, or as Thomas Aquinas, wasted by scholastic vigils, the affection of sleep seemed rather a network of aerial gossammer than of earthly cobwebs – more like a golden haze falling upon him gently from the heavens than cloud exhaling upwards from the flesh.

Then, suddenly, he would wake and chant: 'Diddle, dumpling, my son John went to bed with his breeches on' before dropping off again. The chant could be repeated several times in an evening. A tiny man, Lamb was often carried home slung across someone's back, like a sack of coal.

Coleridge and Lamb were friends at school and the friendship continued after they left. The two – presumably before Coleridge turned to opium – spent many lively evenings at the Salutation and Cat in Newgate Street, enjoying egg-nog and high-minded discussions of literature and philosophy.

Something of Lamb's charm is caught in the following extract from a letter he wrote to a friend, the Rev. Henry Cary, with whom he had dined and, apparently, grown a little merry.

> I protest I know not in what words to invest myself of the shameful violation of hospitality, which I was guilty of on that fateful Thursday. Let it be blotted from the calendar. Had it been committed at a layman's house, say a merchant's or manufacturer's, a cheesemonger's or greengrocer's, or, to go higher, a barrister's, a member of Parliament's, a rich banker's, I should felt alleviation, a drop of self-pity. But to be seen deliberately to go out of the house of a clergyman drunk! A clergyman of the Church of England too!

Lamb tried to drink less from time to time, as his tolerance to alcohol was limited. He wrote of the morning after: 'My head is playing all the tunes in the world, ringing such peals! it has just finished the "Merry Christ Church Bells" and absolutely is beginning "Turn again Whittington", buz, buz, buz, bum, bum, bum, wheeze, wheeze, feu, feu, tinky, tinky.' He even attempted temperance briefly but he enjoyed conviviality too much, loved 'the glorious care-drowning night, that heals all our wrongs, pours wine into our mortifications, changes the scene from indifferent and flat to bright and brilliant'.

Letter to Dr J V Asbury

> It is an observation of a wise man, that 'Moderation is best in all things'. I cannot agree with him 'in liquor'. There is a smoothness and oiliness in wine that makes it go down by a natural Channel, which I am positive was made for that descending. Else, why does not wine choke us? Could nature have made that sloping lane, not to facilitate the down-going? She does nothing in vain. You know that better than I. You know how often she has helped you at a dead lift, and how much better entitled she is to a fee than yourself sometimes, when you carry off the credit. Still, there is something due to manners and customs, and I should apologise to you and Mrs Asbury for being absolutely carried home upon a man's shoulders thro' Silver Street, up Parsons Lane, by the Chapels (which might have taught me better) and then to be deposited

like a dead log at Gaffer Westwood's, who, it seems, does not 'insure' against intoxification. Not that the mode of conveyance is objectionable. On the contrary, it is more easy than a one horse chaise.

Ariel, in the 'Tempest' says:

> On a Bat's back do I fly
> After Sunset merrily.

Now I take it, that Ariel must sometimes have stayed out late of nights. Indeed he pretends that 'where the bee sucks, there lurks he' – as much as to say that his suction is as innocent as that little innocent (but damnably stinging when he is provok'd) winged creature. But I take it, Ariel was fond of metheglin of which the Bees are notorious Brewers. But then you will say, what a shocking sight to see a middle-aged-gentleman-and-a-half riding upon a Gentleman's back up Parsons Lane at midnight. Exactly the time for that sort of conveyance when nobody can see him, nobody but Heaven and his own Conscience; now Heaven makes fools, and don't expect much from her own creation; and as for Conscience, she and I have long since come to a compromise. I have given up false modesty and she allows me to abate a little of the true ... By the way, is magnesia good on these occasions?? 3III pol. med. sum. antenoct. in rub. can. I am no licentiate, but know enough of simples to beg you to send me a draught after this model. But still you'll say (or the men and maids at your house will say) that it is not a seemly sight for an old gentleman to go home a pick-a-back. Well, maybe it is not. But I have never studied grace. I take it to be a mere superficial accomplishment. I regard more the internal acquisitions. The great object after supper is to get home, and whether that is obtained in a horizontal posture, or perpendicular (as foolish men and apes affect for dignity) I think is little to the purpose. The end is always greater than the means. Here I am, able to compose a sensible rational apology, and what signifies how I got here? I have just sense enough to remember I was very happy last night, and to thank our kind host and hostess, and that's Sense enough, I hope. N.B. what is good for a desperate head-ache? why, Patience, and a determination not to mind being miserable all day long. And that I have made my mind up to.

Malcolm Lowry

Complex, inspired, tortured, bizarre – admirers of *Under the Volcano* claim it is the best book about drink and drinkers ever written. It is a bibulous hymn, a eulogy for inebriates. Lowry was a lifelong boozer, drinking prodigious amounts. He had a powerful physique, and needed it – in his student days he boasted of drinking sixteen pints of beer and a half-bottle of whisky in a session, which was probably true.

In London with a friend on an evening's pub-crawl they had an experience that almost sobered them up. Just after closing time they were wandering along Fitzroy Street when, to their disbelief and horror, they saw two large elephants going into Charlotte Street. Concerned that they had reached the stage of seeing pink elephants, they set off in pursuit but the elephants had, predictably, disappeared. But they were relieved to find evidence of their existence in a heap of steaming elephant dung.

During a sojourn in Mexico Lowry discovered the powerful local drinks: mescal, tequila, pulque – all distilled from varieties of the maguey plant – and Mexico's dark beer.

It was clear he had become an alcoholic. At one point in 1949 he admitted drinking an average of at least 2½ to 3 litres of red wine a day, apart from other drinks at bars; on another occasion be talked of downing about 2 litres of rum each day.

Yet he worked at his writing during these massive boozing sessions, had affairs, and maintained a dark sense of humour. He wrote to a friend: 'Very near a mental and nervous collapse, though cheerfulness is always breaking in.' When he was in hospital for an operation for varicose veins in North America he was put in the maternity ward as a temporary measure. He described how an expectant father arrived and was astonished to see him there. Lowry said, 'I explained I was just one of those new, larger, as it were atomic babies just recently on the market.'

Lowry admired Baudelaire and his credo: 'Be always drunken. Nothing else matters: that is the only question. If you would not feel the horrible burden of Time weighing on your shoulders and crushing you to the earth, be drunken continually.' The Consul in *Under the Volcano* echoes these thoughts, as he talks with a woman and thinks about the cantina:

You misunderstand me if you think it is altogether darkness I see, and if you insist on thinking so, how can I tell why I do it? But if you look at the sunlight there, ah, then perhaps you'll get the answer, see, look at the way it falls through the window; what beauty can compare to that of a cantina in the early morning? ... for not even the gates of heaven, opened wide to receive me, could fill me with such celestial complicated and hopeless joy as the iron screen that rolls up with a crash, as the unpadlocked jalousies which admit those whose souls tremble with the drinks they carry unsteadily to their lips.

Under the Volcano

The Consul dropped his eyes at last. How many bottles since then? In how many glasses, how many bottles had he hidden himself, since then alone? Suddenly he saw them, the bottles of aguardiente, of anis, of jerez, of Highland Queen, the glasses, a babel of glasses – towering, like the smoke from the train that day – built to the sky, then falling, the glasses toppling and crashing, falling downhill from the Generalife Gardens, the bottles breaking, bottles of Oporto, tinto, blanco, bottles of Pernod, Oxygénée, absinthe, bottles smashing, bottles cast aside, falling with a thud on the ground in parks, under benches, beds, cinema seats, hidden in drawers at Consulates, bottles of Calvados dropped and broken, or bursting into smithereens, tossed into garbage heaps, flung into the sea, the Mediterranean, the Caspian, the Caribbean, bottles floating in the ocean, dead Scochmen on the Atlantic highlands – and now he saw them, smelt them, all from the very beginning – bottles, bottles, bottles, and glasses, glasses, glasses, of bitter, of Dubonnet, of Falstaff, Rye, Johnny Walker, Vieux Whisky, *blanc* Canadien, the aperitifs, the digestifs, the demis, the dobles, the *noch ein* Herr Obers, the *et glas* Araks, the *tusen taks*, the bottles, the bottles, the beautiful bottles of tequila, and the gourds, gourds, gourds, the millions of gourds of beautiful mescal ... The Consul sat very still. His conscience sounded muffled with the roar of water. It whacked and whined round the wooden frame-house with the spasmodic breeze, massed, with the thunderclouds over the trees, seen through the windows, its factions. How indeed could he hope to find himself to begin again when, somewhere, perhaps, in one of those lost or broken bottles, in one of those glasses, lay, for ever, the solitary clue to his identity? How could he go back and look now, scrabble among the broken glass, under the eternal bars, under the oceans?

... 'All right, Geoffrey: suppose we forget it until you're feeling better: we can cope with it in a day or two, when you're sober.'

'But good lord!'

The Consul sat perfectly still staring at the floor while the enormity of the insult passed into his soul. As if, as if, he were not sober now! Yet there was some elusive subtlety in the impeachment that still escaped him. For he was not sober. No, he was not, not at this very moment he wasn't! But what had that to do with a minute before, or half an hour ago? And what right had Yvonne to assume it, assume either that he was not sober now, or that, far worse, in a day or two he *would* be sober? And even if he were not sober now, by what fabulous stages, comparable indeed only to the paths and spheres of the Holy Cabbala itself, had he reached *this* stage again, touched briefly once before this morning, this stage at which alone he could, as she put it, 'cope', this precarious precious stage, so arduous to maintain, of being drunk in which alone he was sober! What right had she, when he had sat suffering the tortures of the damned and the madhouse on her behalf for fully twenty-five minutes on end without having a decent drink, even to hint that he was anything, but to her eyes, sober? Ah, a woman could not know the perils, the complications, yes, the *importance* of a drunkard's life! From what conceivable standpoint of rectitude did she imagine she could judge what was anterior to her arrival? And she knew nothing whatever of what all too recently he had gone through, his fall in the Calle Nicaragua, his aplomb, coolness, even bravery there – the Burke's Irish whiskey! What a world! And the trouble was she had now spoiled the moment. Because the Consul now felt that he might have been capable, remembering Yvonne's 'perhaps I'll have one after breakfast', and all that implied, of saying, in a minute (but for her remark and yes, in spite of any salvation), 'Yes by all means you are right: let us go!' But who could agree with someone who was so certain you were going to be sober the day after tomorrow? It wasn't as though either, upon the most superficial plane, it were not well known that no one could tell when he was drunk. Just like the Taskersons: God bless them. He was not the person to be seen reeling about in the street. True he might lie down in the street, if need be, like a gentleman, but he would not reel. Ah, what a world it was, that trampled down the truth and drunkards alike! A world full of bloodthirsty people, no less! Bloodthirsty, did I hear you say bloodthirsty, Commander Firmin?

'But my lord, Yvonne, surely you know by this time I can't get drunk however much I drink,' he said almost tragically, taking an abrupt swallow of strychnine. 'Why, do you think I *like* swilling down this awful *nux vomica* or belladonna or whatever it is of Hugh's?' The Consul got up with his empty glass and began to walk around the room. He was not so much aware of having done by default anything fatal (it wasn't as if, for instance, he'd thrown his whole life away) as something merely foolish, and at the same time, as it were, sad. Yet there seemed a call for some amends. He either thought or said:

'Well, tomorrow perhaps I'll drink beer only. There's nothing like beer to straighten you out, and a little more strychnine, and then the next day just beer – I'm sure no one will object if I drink beer. This Mexican stuff is particularly full of vitamins, I gather ... For I can see it really is going to be somewhat of an occasion, this reunion of us all, and then perhaps when my nerves are back to normal again, I'll go off it completely. And then, who knows,' he brought up by the door, 'I might get down to work again and finish my book!'

Samuel Pepys

Two men emerge from the diaries of Samuel Pepys: a highly capable civil servant respected for calm, shrewd judgement; and a deeply sensual character with a fondness for womanizing, wine and play-going. It is a tribute to Pepys's energy and enthusiasm, his intelligence and appetite for life, that he was highly successful in both roles. Affairs of state, court intrigue, budgets and accounts are described side by side with sexual encounters, visits to the theatre and much of draughts of ale, bottles and quarts of wine, liberally quaffed at all times of the day.

He seems never to boast or lie about himself and his doings. A typical day would be morning at the office followed by 'at noon, Sir William Batten, Colonel Slingsby, and I by coach to the Tower, to Sir

John Robinson's, to dinner; where great good cheer ... After dinner, to drink all the afternoon. Towards night the Duchess and ladies went away. Then we set to it again till it was very late.'

There were, inevitably, consequences from these events: 'My head aching all day from last night's debauch'. Help was at hand, in the tradition of 'the hair of the dog', however: 'At noon dined with Sir W Batten and Pen, who would have me drink two good draughts of sack today to cure me of last night's disease, which I thought strange, but I think find it true.'

Pepys recognized the dangers of the daily temptations of the tavern and resolved to mend his ways. 'Finding my head grow weak nowadays if I come to drink wine, and therefore hope that I shall leave it off of myself, which I pray God I could do.' It was not to be, for a couple of weeks later he records in his diary a pleasant day of playing bowls and making music with friends: 'we stayed talking and singing and drinking great draughts of claret and eating botargo [a kind of sausage] and bread and butter till twelve at night, it being moonshine; and so to bed, very near fuddled.'

One Sunday he admitted that he was 'almost foxed' after too much wine at dinner and supper, so much so he dared not follow his Sabbath custom of reading prayers 'for fear of being perceived by my servants in what case I was'.

He tried for a more sober way of life on many occasions, sometimes succeeding for a time, but had little chance of prolonged success with a life so full of enjoyable things, such as a feast where:

> we had fricasee of rabbits, and chickens, a leg of mutton boiled, three carps in a dish, a great dish of a side of lamb, a dish of roasted pigeons, a dish of four lobsters, three tarts, a lamprey pie, a most rare pie, a dish of anchovies, good wine of several sorts, and all things mighty noble, and to my great content.

Diary

Volume 1, 1660

26 feb. ... by and by Mr Pechell and Sanch and I went out. Pechell to church – Sanchy and I to the Rose tavern where we sat and drank till sermon done; and then Mr Pechell came to us and

we sat drinking the King's and his whole family's health till it began to be dark. Then we parted; Sanch and I went to my lodgings where we found my father and Mr Pierce at the door, and I took them both and Mr Blaydon to the Rose tavern and there gave them a quart or two of wine, not telling them that we had been there before. After that we broke up; my father, Mr Zanch and I to Cosen Angiers for supper where I caused two bottles of wine to be carried from the Rose tavern … After that we sat down and talked; I took leave of all of my friends and so to my Inn … I stayed up a little while, playing the fool with the lass of the house at the door of the chamber; and so to bed.

9 March I could not sleep; and being overheated with drink, I made a promise the next morning to drink no strong drink this week for I find it makes me sweat in bed and puts me quite out of order.

9 August And from thence to the Rhenish wine-house … and sending for my wife we dined there – very merry and after dinner parted. After dinner with my wife to Mrs Blackburne to visit her. She being within I left my wife there; and I to the Privy Seal, where I despatch some business; and from thence to Mrs Blackburne again who did treat my wife and I with great civility and did give us a fine collation of collar of beef &c. Thence, I having my head full of drink through having drunk so much Rhenish wine in the morning and more in the afternoon at Mrs Blackburne. Came home and so to bed, not well; and very ill all night.

10 aug. I had a great deal of pain all night and great looseness upon me so I could not sleep. In the morning I had with much pain and to the office I went and dined at home; and after dinner with great pain in my back I went by water to White-Halle to the Privy Seale …

11 aug. I rose today without any pain, which makes me think that my pain yesterday was nothing but from my drinking too much the day before.

31 May 1669 (final entry)

Had another meeting with the Duke of York, at White Hall, on yesterday's work, and made a good advance: and so, being called by my wife, we to the Park, Mary Batelier, and a Dutch gentleman, a friend of hers, being with us. Then to 'The World's End', a drinking house by the Park; and there merry, and so home late.